Rome: Marble statue of St. Paul in front of St. Peter's Basilica, the Vatican (sculptor, Adamo Tadolini, 1788-1868)

In the Footsteps of the Saints

ST. PAUL'S LAST JOURNEY

OTTO F.A. MEINARDUS

CARATZAS BROTHERS, PUBLISHERS
New Rochelle, New York — 1979

First published in Greece by

Lycabettus Press
P.O. Box 3391
Kolonaki
Athens
Greece

Published in North America by

CARATZAS BROTHERS, PUBLISHERS
246 Pelham Road, New Rochelle,
New York 10805

ISBN: 0-89241-073-6 (hardcover)
ISBN: 0-89241-046-9 (paperback)
Library of Congress Catalog
Card Number 78-51247

CONTENTS

PREFACE

When and where did St. Paul's last journey begin and end? Some people believe that the Apostle's last journey began in Damascus sometime in 35 A.D. when the Lord sent Ananias, a disciple in Damascus, to St. Paul to say "how much he (St. Paul) must suffer for the sake of my name" (Acts 9:16). Others believe St. Paul's last journey began with his departure for Rome from Caesarea on the ship from Adramyttium in the autumn of 61. Early Christian tradition held that St. Paul's last journey was mercifully short, beginning in the Praetorium in Rome and ending with his martyrdom on the Via Ostia at a site later marked by the Three Fountains. If, however, we should have had the opportunity to ask the Apostle in person, he probably would have replied that his last journey began in Corinth, when he ended his three month stay in the Achaian capital. In Corinth he had collected offerings for the poor in Jerusalem (I Cor. 16:1-4, II Cor. 8:1-9:15), in Corinth he had written his longest and most significant letter, to the Romans, in which he set forth his plans about his forthcoming journey to Jerusalem (Rom. 15:25), his hope to visit with the Roman Christians (Rom. 15:30-32), and his desire to carry his mission to Spain (Rom. 15:24, 28).

In this volume we shall trace St. Paul's journeys from Corinth via Jerusalem to Rome, a journey which was an important milestone in the fulfillment of the Apostle's mandate. As a Roman citizen he felt compelled to preach the Gospel of Jesus Christ in the West and and to visit the Eternal

City, the political and administrative center of the ancient world. Many Bible students, following St. Luke's implication in the Acts of the Apostles, have regarded the Apostle's journey to Rome as the climax of his missionary work. For St. Luke the narrative which began in Jerusalem culminated in Rome, where Christianity, mysteriously, already had been established. St. Luke's purpose was to describe the spread of the Church of Jesus Christ from the Mount of Olives to the Tiber. For the Apostle Paul, however, Rome was not the final destination but an important stepping stone for further expansion of Christ's Gospel in the West. St. Paul intended to go to Spain.

We shall follow the steps of the Apostle from the last few weeks of his third missionary journey to Corinth to his martyrdom outside the city walls of Rome, traveling across most of what was the Roman Empire from the eastern to the western shores of the Mediterranean Sea. From the Roman province of Achaia we shall travel east through the provinces of Macedonia and Asia, and then through the eastern Aegean islands, Lycia, and Phoenicia to Jerusalem. From there we shall turn westward via Lycia, Crete, Melite, Sicily, Campania (Puteoli), and Rome, and then on to Tarraconensis in Spain before returning to Rome. The period of St. Paul's last journey extends from the year 59 to 67, when Nero occupied the imperial throne and Agrippa II, the last king of the family of Herod the Great, ruled over the northern tetrarchies.

As in my two earlier volumes on St. Paul, *St. Paul in Greece* and *St. Paul in Ephesus and the Cities of Galatia and Cyprus,* I have relied upon St. Luke's narrative in the Acts of the Apostles. Since in my view the Apostle's last journey began in Corinth, I have followed the Evangelist's record in Acts 20:2-28:31. Wherever possible I have turned to St. Paul's personal testimony as contained in his letters to the young churches. Furthermore, I have consulted the contemporary Greek, Roman, and Jewish writers to place the Biblical story in its geographical and historical setting. Over the past few years I have visited all the Pauline sites mentioned in the Acts of the Apostles and by the Fathers of the Early Church. In doing so I did not have the advantage, as did St. Paul, of traveling within the borders of one empire, for on such a journey the 20th century Bible student crosses a minimum of nine national borders (Israel, Lebanon, Syria, Turkey, Greece, Yugoslavia, Malta, Italy, Spain).

This book necessarily has to deal with two controversial issues: the location of St. Paul's shipwreck and the life of the Apostle after St. Luke's account abandons him in Rome. I shall turn first to the site of St. Paul's shipwreck, which is only one of the many Christian Holy Places whose authenticity is not universally accepted.

A faith maintaining that God reveals Himself in time and space always has believers who wish to enshrine the mighty acts of God. The issue of the Christian Holy Places is intimately associated with man's apparent need to commune with God or to venerate His Holy Apostles in certain places believed to be hallowed by some religiously significant act as recorded in the Holy Scriptures or in the traditions of the Church. Both churchmen and scholars often disagree concerning precisely where certain events occurred, and the disagreements have sadly affected both the devotional climate for believers and the purely academic quest for accuracy. Christian pilgrims to the Holy Land have long been exposed to several rival claims held by members of the Sacred Congregations belonging to the same Communion. For the Franciscans the Via Dolorosa in Jerusalem, with its fourteen stations, leads from the Antonia Fortress to the Church of the Holy Sepulchre, while Dominican scholars of the École Biblique in Jerusalem have convincingly argued that the Via Dolorosa began at Herod's Palace. The site of the first station obviously depends upon where Pontius Pilate stayed during that particular Passover season, and this we do not know. The Franciscans believe that the Risen Christ appeared to the two disciples in Emmaus al-Qubaibah, while the Dominicans, following the testimonies of Origen, Eusebius, and St. Jerome, believe that this occurred in Emmaus Amwas. Most Christians believe that Mount Tabor (Jabal at-Tur) was the site of the Transfiguration of Our Lord, yet many Christians maintain that the event occurred on Mount Hermon (Jabal ash-Sheikh). Catholics believe that Our Lord instituted the Last Supper on Mount Zion where the Cenacle commemorates this event, but the Syrian Orthodox hold that their Patriarchate of St. Mark was built on the site of the home of John Mark, where the Last Supper was celebrated. Greek, Armenian, and some Catholic believers hold to the tradition that the Holy Virgin fell asleep in Jerusalem, where her tomb is shown in the Valley of Jehosaphat, while other Catholics maintain that she spent the last days of her life in Ephesus.

Sites pertaining to events in the lives of Jesus Christ and the Virgin Mary are not the only ones without agreed locations. A wealth of traditions has developed around the locations associated with the ministry of the Holy Apostles, including, of course, St. Paul. In Crete, for example, the Christians of Loutro, a few miles west of Sphakia, believe that the Apostle landed and baptized his first Cretan converts there, and the people of Hierapetra in the 17th century claimed the same honor for a site near their city. In an attempt to be fair to both the Croatian and Maltese Christians regarding their traditions and beliefs concerning the site of St. Paul's shipwreck, I have included a description of the sites in both Yugoslavia and Malta.

Many Bible students have asked what happened to St. Paul after the end of St. Luke's account in the Acts of the Apostles. St. Luke concludes his narrative on the abrupt, triumphal note that, while in Rome, the Apostle preached the Kingdom of God and taught about the Lord Jesus Christ openly and unhindered (Acts 28:31). What was the outcome of St. Paul's appeal to Caesar? It has been argued that St. Luke stopped so abruptly because he wrote the book to document the dramatic expansion of the Christian faith from the Mount of Olives to the Roman Forum, and that he considered the task completed as soon as he had written of St. Paul in the capital of the Roman Empire. Furthermore, if the Acts of the Apostles were written at least in part to demonstrate to the Roman officials the compatibility of the Christian faith with the laws of the empire, an account of St. Paul's appearance before a tribunal, followed by his conviction and martyrdom would have been self defeating. We may never know for certain what happened to St. Paul after the two years in Rome. Commenting on the Acts of the Apostles, St. John Chrysostom wrote, "At this point the historian stops his account and leaves the reader thirsting so that thereafter he guesses for himself."

Ever since the latter part of the first century Christians have been doing just that. Some scholars, basing their theories upon references in the Pastoral Epistles, maintain that, after his release, perhaps because the case against him fell by default, St. Paul traveled again to the East. They argue that St. Paul may have visited Ephesus and Macedonia (I Tim. 1:3), Troas (II Tim. 4:13), Crete (Titus 1:5), and Nicopolis (Titus 3:12). I do not wish to enter the scholarly debates concerning the authenticity of the three Pastoral Epistles (I and II Timothy, and Titus), but I recognize the many difficulties in relying upon these letters as sources of information about the Apostle's life after his first Roman imprisonment. A visit to Spain by St. Paul is, however, implied by St. Clement of Rome in his letter to the Corinthians, and other 2nd century writers believe that St. Paul visited Spain. Following their lead, I submit that, after the Apostle stayed two years in Rome, he may have made a missionary journey to Spain after which he returned to Rome where he was martyred in 67 A.D. during the Neronian persecutions.

In an unprecedented manner, Biblical studies since the mid-20th century have turned to the Apostle of the Gentiles. This may be partly because of the situational nature of his letters and their relevance to our modern problems. We are also newly aware of what we can learn of early Christianity by studying the apostolic communities through the eyes of their founder and shepherd. In addition, the 19th centenary celebrations in the 1950's and 1960's in Athens, Corinth, Malta, Rome, and Tarragona have stimulated interest in the Apostle's life and message. I hope that this study, as my earlier *St. Paul in Greece* and *St. Paul in Ephesus and the Cities of Galatia and Cyprus,* will help the religiously oriented visitor to the Mediterranean world to better understand St. Paul's task and message.

The Scripture quotations in this book are from the Revised Standard Version of the Bible, copyrighted 1946 and 1952 by the Division of Christian Education of the National Council of Churches of Christ in the U.S.A., and are used by permission. I acknowledge with gratitude the financial assistance from Mr. Evangelos Syrigos which enabled me to make some of the journeys necessary to complete this study. I am thankful for the suggestions and help received from my colleagues at the American School of Classical Studies in Athens, the Benedictine Fathers of the Monastery of Montserrat near Barcelona, the Franciscan Friars of St. Paul's Bay in Malta, the Sisters of St. Elizabeth in Rome, and many members of the clergy in Dubrovnik, Beirut, Damascus, and Jerusalem. I also thank Dr. Hendrik Morsman, whose patient developing of my pictures has much improved the illustrations.

Paros, Cyclades, 1975   Otto F. A. Meinardus

THE END FORESHADOWED

From Corinth to Miletus

(Paul) came to Greece. There he spent three months, and when a plot was made against him by the Jews as he was about to sail for Syria, he determined to return through Macedonia. Sopater of Beroea, the son of Pyrthus, accompanied him; and of the Thessalonians, Aristarchus and Secundus; and Gaius of Derbe, and Timothy; and the Asians, Tychicus and Trophimus. These went on and were waiting for us at Troas, but we sailed away from Philippi after the days of Unleavened Bread, and in five days we came to them at Troas, where we stayed for seven days. On the first day of the week, when we were gathered together to break bread, Paul talked with them, intending to depart on the morrow; and he prolonged his speech until midnight. There were many lights in the upper chamber where we were gathered. And a young man named Eutychus was sitting in the window. He sank into a deep sleep as Paul talked still longer; and being overcome by sleep, he fell down from the third story and was taken up dead. But Paul went down and bent over him, and embracing him said, "Do not be alarmed, for his life is in him." And when Paul had gone up and had broken bread and eaten, he conversed with them a long while, until daybreak, and so departed. And they took the lad away alive, and were not a little comforted.

But going ahead to the ship, we set sail for Assos, intending to take Paul aboard there; for so he had

Corinth: Temple of Apollo, 6th century B.C., with the medieval fortifications on Acrocorinth in the background (Acts 20:2)

arranged, intending himself to go by land. And when he met us at Assos, we took him on board and came to Mitylene. And sailing from there we came the following day opposite Chios; the next day we touched at Samos; and the day after that we came to Miletus. For Paul had decided to sail past Ephesus, so that he might not have to spend time in Asia; for he was hastening to be at Jerusalem, if possible, on the day of Pentecost.

Acts 20:2-16

Strictly speaking, St. Paul's last journey began in Corinth, the capital of the Roman province of Achaia. The Apostle was deeply involved, both personally and spiritually, in the trials and triumphs of the Corinthian Christians who had remained close to his heart for many years. His first visit to Corinth, which lasted 18 months, began in the spring of 50. Four years later, while living in Ephesus, he revisited Corinth to settle congregational disputes which threatened the unity of the young church (II Cor. 13:2). He paid his last visit to Corinth during the winter months of 55 and 56. At that time the church in Corinth was healthy, and St. Paul was able, undisturbed, to prepare his mission to the West. St. Paul composed his letter to the Romans, the most important Christian theological treatise ever written, during this last visit to Corinth. In addition, he wrote a brief introductory letter for "sister Phoebe, a deaconess of the church at Cenchreae," to the members of the church in Ephesus (Rom. 16). This letter of greetings mentions as co-workers Priscilla and Aquila; Epaenetus, the first convert in Asia for Christ; Andronicus; Junius, with whom St. Paul was imprisoned in Ephesus; and many others. During this time the Apostle stayed in the house belonging to Gaius, who had come from Derbe in Asia Minor and whom St. Paul had baptized during his first visit to Corinth (I Cor. 1:14).

St. Paul's ministry in Corinth is commemorated by the impressive new cathedral in the modern city of Corinth. Every year on June 29, the feast of SS. Peter and Paul, a vesper service is conducted by the Metropolitan of Corinth at the traditional *bema* in the ruins of Old Corinth.

Although he wanted to travel west, St. Paul had to return to Jerusalem before he could visit Rome and Spain. For several years he had been collecting funds for the support of the poor in Jerusalem as he had promised James, Peter, and John in Jerusalem when they extended their right hands in fellowship to him as Apostle to the Gentiles (Gal. 2:9-10). He strongly felt that the Gentile churches were pleased to make this contribution "and, indeed, they are in debt to them (the Jerusalem Christians), for if the Gentiles have come to share in their spiritual blessings, they ought also to be of service to them in material blessings" (Rom. 15:27). Furthermore, St. Paul thought that the gift would help reconcile the rift between the Jerusalem and the Gentile churches. With this purpose in mind, the Apostle had no alternative but to go to Jerusalem himself, for no one else could have delivered the money and its message so effectively.

As his letter to the Romans clearly shows, however, he was reluctant to sail eastward because he foresaw his serious difficulties with the elders of the Jerusalem church. He was sufficiently concerned that he asked for intercessory prayer: "I appeal to you, brethren, by our Lord Jesus Christ and by the love of the Spirit, to strive together with me in your prayers to God on my behalf, that I may be delivered from the unbelievers in Judea and that my service for Jerusalem may be acceptable to the saints, so that by God's will I may come to you with joy and be refreshed in your company" (Rom. 15:30-32). Events justified the Apostle's fears (Acts 21:27 ff.).

St. Paul planned to visit Syria on his way to Jerusalem, but just as he was leaving (probably while in the port of Cenchreae), he discovered that "a plot was made against him by the Jews" (Acts 20:3) and, in the words of the Western Text of the Bible, "the Holy Spirit told him to return through Macedonia." Visiting Macedonia enabled him to revisit and strengthen the churches from which he had collected the funds. He was accompanied by several of his disciples, including Sopater of Beroea, who was probably the Sosipater

3

mentioned in Rom. 16:21 along with Timothy and Lucius. If Lucius is assumed to be Luke, and Timothy St. Paul's faithful lieutenant, then this same trio had accompanied St. Paul from Corinth, where he had written the letter introducing the deaconess Phoebe to the Ephesians, a letter which includes greetings from these three companions.

In Thessalonica the travelers were joined by Aristarchus, Secundus, and Gaius, but the whole group did not cross together from Europe to Asia, for St. Paul and St. Luke stayed in Philippi while the others preceded them to Troas. The church in Philippi had a special claim on St. Paul's attention, for its members had supported him while he was in prison in Ephesus and he had sent very personal messages, as contained in his letter to the Philippians, to them. Since the Feast of the Unleavened Bread was at hand he stayed with them longer than he had planned, undoubtedly reminding the Jewish Christians in Philippi, as he had the Corinthians, of the Christian significance of the Jewish Passover. For St. Paul it was no longer a Jewish ceremony, but Christ was the Passover Who had been sacrificed.

> Cleanse out the old leaven that you may be a new lump, as you really are unleavened. For Christ, our paschal lamb, has been sacrificed. Let us, therefore, celebrate the festival, not with the old leaven, the leaven of malice and evil, but with the unleavened bread of sincerity and truth.
>
> I Cor. 5:7-8

Once the Passover moon was waning, St. Paul and St. Luke sailed for Troas. The distance between Neapolis and Troas usually could be covered in two days, but unfavorable winds made the trip last five days. St. Paul had visited Troas before, but on both occasions he was prevented from staying any length of time. On his first visit to Troas "a vision appeared to Paul in the night: a man of Macedonia was standing beseeching him and saying, 'Come over to Macedonia and help us'" (Acts 16:9), and on his second visit,

4

though "a door was opened" for him and he had gathered a congregation to preach the Gospel of Christ, his impatience to see his brother Titus soon compelled him to leave (II Cor. 2:12-13). This time St. Paul was able to strengthen the church in Troas. We assume that the congregation met in Alexandria Troas, the port city founded by Antigonus and Lysimachus at the command of Alexander the Great. Because of its artificial harbor, Alexandria Troas had become a powerful commercial center, of which, however, no significant remains survive.

We do not know what the Apostle did during his first six days in the city. We do have, however, an account of a Christian service on St. Paul's last day, when the congregation gathered to break bread on the Lord's day (Acts 20:7), which began on Saturday at 6 P.M. The Christians of Troas had assembled in an upper room to celebrate the Meal, which their Lord Jesus Christ had enjoined on all His disciples. St. Paul, knowing he would not meet with them again, preached until midnight. One of the listeners, a young man named Eutychus who was sitting in a window, sank into a deep sleep and fell three stories down to the ground. Although the Western Text of the Bible refers to St. Paul's traveling companion Tychicus as Eutychus, it does not seem likely that this young man Eutychus was one of the companions of the Apostle (Acts 20:4). At first everyone thought the young man was dead, but St. Paul, following the example of his Master (Matt. 9:24, Mark 5:39), said to the congregation: "Do not be alarmed, for his life is in him" (Acts 20:10). With thankful hearts the Apostle and the congregation ate and conversed until dawn.

St. Paul's companions sailed from Troas around the promontory of Lectum to Assos. The Apostle, however, walked the 25 km., roughly half the distance of the sea route. This choice enabled him to stay for a few more hours with his friends in Troas. From II Timothy 4:13 we learn that St. Paul left in Troas his cloak, some books, and parchments, which his traveling companions might well have forgotten to put aboard the ship. As he walked alone along the Roman road to Assos he was undoubtedly aware of the difficulties awaiting him in

Jerusalem. In fact, he may have chosen this opportunity to be by himself to pray to his Heavenly Father for comfort and strength.

St. Paul entered the hilltop town of Assos along the Sacred Way, flanked by numerous tombs of the Hellenistic and Roman periods. Once in the town there was no further delay, and the Apostle and his company sailed southward along the eastern shore of Mitylene (ancient Lesbos). The ship anchored during the night, probably in the capital of Sappho's island, for "on the following day" they passed the island of Chios before touching Samos and arriving at Miletus.

With the Ephesian Elders in Miletus

And from Miletus he sent to Ephesus and called to him the elders of the church. And when they came to him, he said to them:

"You yourselves know how I lived among you all the time from the first day that I set foot in Asia, serving the Lord with all humility and with tears and with trials which befell me through the plots of the Jews; how I did not shrink from declaring to you anything that was profitable, and teaching you in public and from house to house, testifying both to Jews and to Greeks of repentance to God and of faith in our Lord Jesus Christ. And now, behold, I am going to Jerusalem, bound in the spirit, not knowing what shall befall me there; except that the Holy Spirit testifies to me in every city that imprisonment and afflictions await me. But I do not account my life of any value nor as precious to myself, if only I may accomplish my course and the ministry which I received from the Lord Jesus, to testify to the gospel of the grace of God. And now, behold, I know that all you among whom I have gone about preaching the kingdom will see my face no more. Therefore I testify to you this day that I am innocent of the blood of all of you, for I did not shrink from declaring to you the whole counsel of God. Take heed to yourselves and to all the flock, in which the Holy Spirit has made you guardians, to feed the church of the Lord which he obtained for himself with his own blood. I know that after my departure fierce wolves will come in among you, not sparing the flock; and from among your own selves will arise men speaking perverse things, to draw away the disciples after them. Therefore be alert, remembering that for three years I did not cease night or day to admonish every one with tears. And now I commend you to God and to the word of his grace, which is able to build you up and to give you the inheritance among all those who are sanctified. I coveted no one's silver or gold or apparel. You yourselves know that these hands ministered to my necessities, and to those who were with me. In all things I have shown you that by so toiling one must help the weak, remembering the words of the Lord Jesus, how he said, 'It is more blessed to give than to receive.' "

And when he had spoken thus, he knelt down and prayed with them all. And they all wept and embraced Paul and kissed him, sorrowing most of all because of the word he had spoken, that they should see his face no more. And they brought him to the ship.

Acts 20:17-38

The main reason St. Paul did not stop in Ephesus was so he could proceed as quickly as possible to Jerusalem, in time for the Feast of Pentecost, also known as the Feast of the Weeks, or Shebhuoth. This was a day of rejoicing, originally set aside to commemorate the first fruits of the wheat harvest

7

but later celebrated in commemoration of the revelation of the Law in Sinai. St. Paul wanted to be in Jerusalem for this feast in order to demonstrate his loyalty to his Jewish heritage. Since he had spent several years in Ephesus, returning there would have meant involvement with both friends and enemies, and he did not wish to risk the time. Instead, he invited the Ephesian elders to a quiet spot on the outskirts of Miletus for a meeting, which was one of the most touching episodes recorded by St. Luke. He reminded the elders of the opposition from the Ephesian Jews which had caused him tears, trials, and imprisonment. Now he was on his way to Jerusalem expecting more serious difficulties. He was deeply concerned about heretics and schismatics in Ephesus, and he admonished the elders to remain alert, commending them to God. During this meeting St. Paul quoted a saying of Jesus, "It is more blessed to give than to receive" (Acts 20:35), which is not recorded in the Gospels,

Miletus: The Roman theatre (Acts 20:15)

and the question arises whether the Apostle was quoting from a collection of Jesus' sayings or whether these words should be seen as his own summary of his Lord's teachings. When St. Paul finished speaking, he and the Ephesian elders knelt down on the shore and offered prayers to God. The elders grieved that they would see his face no more, and they all realized the difficulties awaiting the Apostle in Jerusalem. They wept, embraced and kissed him, and then accompanied him to the ship.

Miletus, at the mouth of the Meander (Menderes) River, was one of the oldest and most prominent settlements in Ionia. The river has deposited much silt over the ages, and today the remains lie in the middle of a plain. The city was the birthplace of such notable men as Thales, one of the legendary seven wise men, his student Anaximander, and Anaximander's student Anaximenes. Strabo informs us that Miletus had four harbors, of which one could hold an entire fleet. The ship carrying the Apostle would have docked in Lion's Bay, named after the lion monument near the port. The synagogue of Miletus was situated at the southwest corner of the harbor stoa, near the Grattius monument. The existence of a Jewish congregation in this port city is also indicated by an inscription on one of the steps of the city's large theater. This colossal theater, standing 140 meters wide and 30 meters high on the seashore, must have been extremely impressive. First built in the 4th century B.C., it was enlarged several times. During St. Paul's visit to Miletus it could seat more than 15,000 people.

We have no record of a Christian community in Miletus, but some Miletans probably heard St. Paul proclaim the Gospel during his stay in Ephesus.

From Miletus to Caesarea

And when we had parted from them and set sail, we came by a straight course to Cos, and the next day to Rhodes, and from there to Patara. And having found a ship crossing to Phoenicia, we went aboard, and set sail. When we had come in sight of Cyprus, leaving it on the left we sailed to Syria, and landed at Tyre; for there the ship was to unload its cargo. And having sought out the disciples, we stayed there for seven days. Through the Spirit they told Paul not to go on to Jerusalem. And when our days there were ended, we departed and went on our journey; and they all, with wives and children, brought us on our way till we were outside the city; and kneeling down on the beach we prayed and bade one another farewell. Then we went on board the ship, and they returned home.

When we had finished the voyage from Tyre, we arrived at Ptolemais; and we greeted the brethren and stayed with them for one day. On the morrow we departed and came to Caesarea; and we entered the house of Philip the evangelist, who was one of the seven, and stayed with him. And he had four unmarried daughters, who prophesied. While we were staying for some days, a prophet named Agabus came down from Judea. And coming to us he took Paul's girdle and bound his own feet and hands, and said, "Thus says the Holy Spirit, 'So shall the Jews at Jerusalem bind the man who owns this girdle and deliver him into the hands of the Gentiles.' " When we heard this, we and the people there begged him not to go up to Jerusalem. Then Paul answered, "What are you doing, weeping and breaking my heart? For I am ready not only to be imprisoned but

Cos: The Asklepium, 4th century B.C. (Acts 21:1)

even to die at Jerusalem for the name of the Lord Jesus." And when he would not be persuaded, we ceased and said, "The will of the Lord be done."

Acts 21:1-14

After sailing all day the travelers arrived in the evening, probably in the town of Cos on the northeast shore of the island of the same name. The island was famous in antiquity for its Asklepium where Hippocrates (460-357 B.C.) taught, finally dying at the age of 104. St. Luke the physician, who accompanied the Apostle, must have reflected with gratitude upon the achievements of the father of medicine as the ship lay at anchor off the city. He may also have known of his fellow physician, Xenophon of Cos, who is thought to have used his medical knowledge to help Agrippina poison her husband, the emperor Claudius (41-54 A.D.). An inscription mentioning Xenophon of Cos is exhibited in the Antiquarium of Cos. The Christians of Cos commemorated the Apostle's brief visit by dedicating a basilica, today in ruins, to him at Zipari, about 7 km. west of the city of Cos.

From Cos the ship sailed to Rhodes, and as it entered the harbor St. Paul would have seen the remains of the Colossus, one of the Seven Wonders of the ancient world. This impressive bronze monument was built between 304 and 284 B.C., but collapsed during an earthquake in 225 B.C. It stood between 90 and 120 feet tall and weighed close to 250 tons. According to Strabo, the colossus was broken at the knees and, because of an oracle, the people of Rhodes did not attempt to raise it again. Unfortunately, we have no archaeological evidence indicating where the Colossus stood, but a Rhodian tradition asserts that it stood on the site of St. Paul's Gate. Its remains were sold in 656 A.D. by Mu'awiyah, the first 'Umayyad caliph, to a Jewish merchant of Emesa, Syria, who used 900 camels to cart the pieces way.

The Rhodians maintain that the Apostle came ashore and preached the Gospel, bringing many people to the new faith. They also believe that before he left, St. Paul appointed

Prochorus, one of the seven deacons (Acts 6:5), bishop of the island. Prochorus was succeeded by Ephranoras and then by Photinas. Another local tradition, held in Lindos on the southeast coast of the island, has the Apostle's ship arrive at the island in the small harbor at the foot of the acropolis of Lindos, where for centuries pilgrims worshiped Athena Lindia. To this day the small harbor is referred to as "St. Paul's Harbor" and a small barrel vaulted chapel of St. Paul near the shore commemorates the landing and the preaching of the Apostle.

The patron saint of the Rhodians is St. Silas, a prophet and a leader among the brethren (Acts 15:22-32). Rhodian tradition relates how St. Silas's message was doubted by the villagers of Sorone, 25 km. southwest of the capital, until he demonstrated the power of Jesus Christ by healing a paralytic. The villagers thereupon accepted the Christian faith and built a church in honor of their patron.

From Rhodes the ship crossed to the southern shore of Asia Minor to Patara, the port of the city of Xanthus, which stood on the left bank of the Xanthus River. The small bay of Patara is now completely sanded up and the only remains of this former Lycian port, with its famous temple and oracle of the Lycian Apollo, are the ruins of the theater, the Roman bath, and a monumental gate with a triple arch. The 8th century bishop of Eichstadt, St. Willibald, stopped in Patara on his way to the Holy Land, but "the icy winter made the waters rough, and they waited in Patara for the mildness of spring." In the 14th century the city was believed to be the birthplace of St. Nicholas and, although it had been destroyed by the Turks, it was visited by western pilgrims.

The Western Text of the Acts of the Apostles adds that the ship sailed as far as Myra (the modern Turkish village of Demre), which is likely because Myra, famous for its 4th century B.C. Lycian tombs, served as a port of call for the larger ships (Acts 27:5-6). If we accept the account of the apocryphal Acts of Paul and Thecla, which mentions the Apostle's visit to Myra in connection with his first missionary journey and his healing of Hermocrates and Hermippus, then

St. Paul was familiar with this Lycian port. In the Christian world Myra reached fame through its 4th century bishop St. Nicholas, whose generosity and kindness are remembered annually during the Christmas season. The legend of his surreptitious bestowal of dowries upon the three daughters of an impoverished citizen of Myra led to the identification of St. Nicholas with the giving of presents in secret. The Church of St. Nicholas in Myra is a three aisled basilica which was restored in the 11th century. Some of its wall paintings are still visible in the dome.

The Apostle and his companions were fortunate enough to find a large cargo ship about to sail for Phoenicia, and thus were able to continue their journey without delay. With

Safra: Local tradition asserts that the Apostle's ship stopped in Junieh Bay, near the village of Safra, on the way from Patara to Tyre (Acts 21:1-3)

favorable winds the crossing could have been made in 48 hours, passing Cyprus to port before reaching Tyre. In the 1st century A.D. Tyre was neither the prosperous city described by the prophets Isaiah (chapter 23) and Ezekiel (chapters 26 and 27) nor the provincial southern Lebanese coastal town of Sûr which it is today. Ancient Tyre was captured by Alexander the Great after a prolonged siege, but the city lived on under the Seleucids. Because of its distinguished history the Romans bestowed upon it the privileges of a free city, and in St. Paul's time it still served as a commercial center from which Phoenician glass and purple were exported to the West. It is likely that the cargo ship in which St. Paul sailed was carrying grain from the Black Sea or wine from the Greek Islands.

As soon as the ship docked St. Paul went to find the Christians in Tyre, with whom he stayed for seven days. We do not know when and by whom the church of Tyre was founded, though the Apostle evidently knew of the presence of Christians. Probably the Tyrian church had its origin several years before, when those "who were scattered because of the persecution that arose over Stephen traveled as far as Phoenicia . . . speaking the word to none except Jews" (Acts 11:19). St. Paul and St. Barnabas probably had visited the Tyrian Christians on their way from Antioch as "they passed through both Phoenicia and Samaria" (Acts 15:3) to attend the council in Jerusalem. In the apocryphal Acts of Paul it is recorded that "when Paul entered unto Tyre there came a multitude of Jews to him, and they heard of the mighty works. And Paul cast out evil spirits and when the multitude saw this, by the power of God, they praised Him, Who had (given such power) unto Paul." The apocryphal Acts of Paul also report that, while in Tyre, St. Paul healed a youth who was born dumb.

As had the Antiochene congregation (Acts 13:1), so the Tyran church had prophets among its members, some of whom spoke "through the spirit" to warn the Apostle not to go to Jerusalem. But St. Paul was determined to fulfill his mission without regard for his own fears or the advice of his

15

fellow Christians. His departure from Tyre was similar to his departure from Miletus, for the disciples and their families accompanied him through the city gate to the beach where they knelt and prayed for God's blessings upon the Apostle's mission.

From Tyre St. Paul sailed south, either in the same ship or in some smaller, coastal vessel, to Ptolemais (modern Acre), a journey of some 25 km. The Apostle went ashore and visited with the brethren of the local congregation, which would have been founded at the same time as the church in Tyre. Ptolemais, halfway between Tyre in the north and Caesarea in the south, was older than either of the other two cities. Its Old Testament name was Acco, a town of the tribe of Asher (Judges 1:31). During the reign of the Ptolemies it

Acre: The harbor (Acts 21:7)

was known as Ptolemais, and early in the Christian era it was named Colonia Claudii Caesaris in honor of the emperor Claudius. The city gained fame during the Crusades, when it became one of the principal bulwarks of the Christian presence. In the latter part of the 12th century the Crusaders, expelled from Jerusalem, established the capital of the Latin Kingdom in Acre. Because of the importance of the Order of St. John, the city took the name of St. John of Acre. Modern Acre, with the ruins of its outer medieval port and its calm inner harbor, has preserved its eastern appearance better than any other town in the region. Most of the people who live in the old town behind the walls near the sea are Arabs, while most of the people living in the new town to the east are Jewish.

After spending the day with the brethren the Apostle and his companions sailed for Caesarea, some 50 km. south of Ptolemais, where they stayed in the house of Philip the Evangelist. Philip had preached the Gospel even before the Good News was made known to St. Paul on the Damascus Road. He had been very successful in Samaria, for "the multitudes with one accord gave heed to what was said by Philip, when they heard him and saw the signs which he did" (Acts 8:6). This mission was the first definite approach of the Christian Gospel into territory not controlled by Orthodox Jews. Later he converted and baptized the Ethiopian eunuch on the desert road from Jerusalem to Gaza, preached in Azotus (called Ashdod in I Sam. 5:1-6) and in "all the towns" (Acts 8:40), which may have included Lydda and Joppa, before settling in Caesarea, the residence of the Roman procurator of Judaea (Acts 8:26-40). Philip had four unmarried daughters who prophesied and may well have spoken of the perils the Apostle faced in his mission to Jerusalem.

Whether they did or not, the wandering prophet Agabus of Judaea certainly foretold what awaited the Apostle. Agabus's powers were well known because some years earlier he had "foretold by the Spirit that there would be a great famine over all the world; and this took place in the days of

Claudius" (41-54 A.D.) (Acts 11:28). This famine is described by the historians Tacitus and Suetonius. When St. Paul was in Caesarea, Agabus went to him and warned him of the personal danger he faced. Agabus dramatized his prophecy by binding his feet and hands with St. Paul's girdle and saying "so shall the Jews at Jerusalem bind the man who owns this girdle and deliver him into the hands of the Gentiles" (Acts 21:11). St. Paul's companions reacted with tears, imploring him not to go to Jerusalem, but the Apostle was committed to his plans and declared his readiness not only to be imprisoned but even to die in Jerusalem for the sake of the Lord Jesus. His friends finally agreed, putting their sorrow and frustration in the hands of the Lord by saying, "The will of the Lord be done" (Acts 21:14).

In the middle of the 1st century Caesarea was still a young city, for it was only in 25 B.C. that Herod the Great began developing its bay into a seaport, constructing a magnificent city which he dedicated to Caesar Augustus. The new city's administrative and military importance came to surpass that of Jerusalem, as is shown by Vespasian being proclaimed emperor in Caesarea a year after St. Paul's martyrdom in Rome (67 A.D.). St. Paul was held a prisoner for two years in this city (59-61 A.D.). The civil strife which erupted here between the Greeks and the Jews was the main spark for the outbreak of the Jewish War in 66 A.D. The ecclesiastical council of 195 A.D., which decreed that Easter should always be kept on Sunday, convened in Caesarea. The Arabs occupied the city in 640 as did the Crusaders, led by Baldwin I, in 1101. Among the numerous Crusader buildings archaeologists unearthed the remains of a three aisled basilica which was dedicated to St. Paul. William of Tyre recorded that when King Baldwin I occupied the city the Holy Grail, a glass bowl believed to have been used by Jesus Christ at the Last Supper, was found. The Crusaders transferred the Holy Grail to Genoa where it is preserved in the Cathedral of St. Lorenzo.

Caesarea was enclosed by three walls: the outer or Byzantine wall, the Roman wall, and the Herodian or inner

18

wall. East of the Herodian port are the ruins of the Temple of Augustus and the Herodian palace where St. Paul was held prisoner. For several years the archaeological remains of Caesarea have attracted many visitors. The 2nd century A.D.

Caesarea: Copy of the original Pontius Pilate inscription now in the museum in Jerusalem. "Tibericum [Pon]tius Pilatus [Praef]ectus Iuda[eae]"

Roman theater on the seashore, excavated in 1961, has been restored and is now used for musical and theatrical performances.

The famous Pontius Pilate inscription was found during the excavations, giving archaeological confirmation that Pontius Pilate was the procurator under whose administration Jesus Christ was crucified. The ruins of the Caesarean synagogue are close to the Caesarean aqueduct near the shore.

ST. PAUL'S RETURN TO JERUSALEM

From Caesarea to the Temple

After these days we made ready and went up to Jerusalem. And some of the disciples from Caesarea went with us, bringing us to the house of Mnason of Cyprus, an early disciple, with whom we should lodge.

When we had come to Jerusalem, the brethren received us gladly. On the following day Paul went with us to James; and all the elders were present. After greeting them, he related one by one the things that God had done among the Gentiles through his ministry. And when they heard it, they glorified God. And they said to him, "You see, brother, how many thousands there are among the Jews of those who have believed; they are all zealous for the law, and they have been told about you that you teach all the Jews who are among the Gentiles to forsake Moses, telling them not to circumcise their children or observe the customs. What then is to be done? They will certainly hear that you have come. Do therefore what we tell you. We have four men who are under a vow; take these men and purify yourself along with them and pay their expenses, so that they may shave their heads. Thus all will know that there is nothing in what they have been told about you but that you yourself live in observance of the law. But as for the Gentiles who have believed, we have sent a letter with our judgement that they should abstain from what has been sacrificed to idols and from blood and from what is strangled and from unchastity." Then Paul took the men, and the next day he purified himself with them and went into the temple, to give notice when the days of purification would be fulfilled and the offering presented for every one of them.

Acts 21:15-26

The Feast of the Weeks must have been close at hand, for St. Paul and his companions from Macedonia and Asia, accompanied by some of the disciples from Caesarea, went on to Jerusalem. From Caesarea the apostolic party could have traveled along the ancient coastal road past Apollonia to Joppa (modern Jaffa), where St. Peter had raised Tabitha (Acts 9:36-43) and experienced the vision in which God invited him to minister to the Gentiles (Acts 10:1-11:18). From Joppa they would have taken the road eastward through Lydda, where St. Peter had raised Aeneas (Acts 9:32-35), passing the ancient Canaanite settlement of Gezer (Josh. 16:3; I Kings 9:16) the Valley of Sorek, where Delilah lived (Judges 16:4), and Kiriath-jearim (Josh. 15:9) to Jerusalem.

They planned to stay in the house of an early Cypriot Christian named Mnason. We know very little about this early disciple, and both St. Luke and early Christian tradition are silent about the location of his house. Mnason may have accepted the new faith during the lifetime of our Lord Himself for, had he been converted by St. Paul in Cyprus, the Apostle would have known him. He may also have been one of those Cypriot Jews who came to Antioch and "spoke to the Greeks also, preaching the Lord Jesus" (Acts 11:20). According to Cypriot tradition Mnason succeeded Heracleidius as bishop of Tamassus in Cyprus, where he performed many miracles before suffering martyrdom.

Although there is no mention of delivering the collection in Jerusalem, which was one of the main purposes of St. Paul's visit, we may assume that he gave the offering for "the relief of the saints" (II Cor. 8:4) to the Apostle James and all the Jerusalem elders when he met them the day after his arrival. While doing so he may have related the things God had done among the Gentiles, and he probably also reported on his troubles with the Jewish zealots, who had hindered his mission.

Discord and mistrust, however, lurked beneath the cordiality extended to the Apostle. Reports were circulating that St. Paul had not demanded obedience to the Mosaic Law from his Jewish converts in Greece and Asia Minor, and the

22

elders of the Jerusalem church made one last effort to save the situation. They asked the Apostle publicly to demonstrate his loyalty to Mosaic Law and the Temple and, since the Apostle's main objective in visiting Jerusalem was to reconcile the Jerusalem church with the Gentile churches, he agreed. On an earlier occasion he had said, "to the Jews I became as a Jew, in order to win Jews; to those under the law I became as one under the law — though not being myself under the law — that I might win those under the law" (I Cor. 9:20). At Cenchreae, the eastern harbor of Corinth, he had cut his hair (Acts 18:18) in fulfillment of the Nazarite vow (Numbers 6:5). Now the elders asked St. Paul to join four other Jewish Christians in a Nazarite ceremony of purification and to pay for the necessary sacrifices this entailed. It was a common practice for wealthy Jews to help their poorer brethren perform their religious duties by paying for the sacrifices, and Josephus records that King Herod Agrippa I, to gain popularity with the Jews, used to finance the expenses of Nazarites.

According to the Talmud, the purification period lasted for a minimum of thirty days, during which the Nazarite abstained from wine and left his hair uncut. At the end of this period he sacrificed in the Temple (Numbers 6:13-18), then his hair was cut off and burned on the altar. The offerings required were expensive and one wonders how the Apostle, who had worked with his hands for his daily bread, could have paid the expenses for four Nazarites. Did the assembled elders of the Jerusalem church suggest that a portion of the collection which he had given them be used for this purpose?

On the other hand, it is likely that during the thirty day period of their vow the four Nazarites had experienced some kind of defilement or ritual impurity for which they wanted to atone. They could purify themselves by shaving their heads on the seventh day and offering "two turtledoves or two young pigeons to the priest" (Numbers 6:9-11). This would explain the Apostle's appearance in the Temple for the purification ceremony.

St. Paul had hoped that by performing this ceremony of

23

purification according to Jewish ceremonial law he would convince the Jews opposed to him of his orthodoxy. He also felt that his demonstration would protect the elders from being accused of having welcomed a traitor to Mosaic Law. The celebrations of the Feast of the Weeks had attracted many Jews from the provinces, and the Temple area was crowded with pilgrims, among whom were some Jews from Asia. The Apostle wished to demonstrate his willingness to live according to Jewish Law; he was not to ask the Gentiles to do so. This understanding, written some years previously at the Apostolic Council in Jerusalem (Acts 15:28-29), was reiterated now by the elders.

St. Paul's Arrest in the Temple

When the seven days were almost completed, the Jews from Asia, who had seen him in the temple, stirred up all the crowd, and laid hands on him, crying out, "Men of Israel, help! This is the man who is teaching men everywhere against the people and the law and this place; moreover he also brought Greeks into the temple, and he has defiled this holy place." For they had previously seen Trophimus the Ephesian with him in the city, and they supposed that Paul had brought him into the temple. Then all the city was aroused, and the people ran together; they seized Paul and dragged him out of the temple, and at once the gates were shut. And as they were trying to kill him, word came to the tribune of the cohort that all Jerusalem was in confusion. He at once took soldiers and centurions, and ran down to them; and when they saw the tribune and the soldiers, they stopped beating Paul. Then the tribune came up and arrested him, and ordered him to be bound with two chains. He inquired who he was and what he had done. Some of the crowd shouted one thing, some another; and as he could not learn the facts because of the uproar, he ordered him to be brought into the barracks. And when he came to the steps, he was actually carried by the soldiers because of the violence of the crowd; for the mob of the people followed, crying, "Away with him!"

As Paul was about to be brought into the barracks, he said to the tribune, "May I say something to you?" And he said, "Do you know Greek? Are you not the Egyptian, then, who recently stirred up a revolt and led the four thousand men of the Assassins out into the wilderness?" Paul replied, "I am a Jew, from Tarsus in Cilicia, a citizen of no mean city; I beg you, let me speak to the people." And when he had given him leave, Paul, standing on the steps, motioned with his hand to the people; and when there was a great hush, he spoke to them in the Hebrew language, saying:

"Brethren and fathers, hear the defense which I now make before you."

Acts 21:27-22:1

Although St. Paul had the support of the Jerusalem elders, he was still opposed by many Jews, particularly the zealous Jews from the synagogue of Ephesus who had been irritated by the growth of the Christian church in that city. Many of these Asian Jews had come to Jerusalem for the feast and were angered by seeing St. Paul in the Temple. They had recognized Trophimus, an Ephesian Gentile, and they maintained that St. Paul had brought him into the Temple. These Ephesian Jews may have been the same ones who had encouraged Alexander to speak during the Silversmiths' Riot in the Ephesian theater (Acts 19:33).

The presence of a Gentile in the Temple was a capital offense under Jewish Law, for it polluted the Holy of Holies. The Temple was surrounded by a low stone balustrade on which Greek and Latin inscriptions warned all Gentiles not to advance beyond it on pain of death. Two of these inscriptions,

25

both in Greek, have been found. One of them is exhibited in the Rockefeller Museum in Jerusalem, and another is in the Archaeological Museum in Istanbul. The first was found outside the Jerusalem walls near St. Stephen's Gate in 1935. The second was found by C. Clermont-Ganneau in 1871 in a wall near the Bab al-Atm leading to the Haram ash-Sharif. Translated into English, the text reads:

> Let no one of foreign race proceed within the railing of the precinct in the temple. If anyone is caught, he shall be liable unto himself for his subsequent death.

To better appreciate the situation we will interrupt the narrative and provide some information about the Temple at the time of St. Paul's visit. Herod the Great, grandson of an Idumean convert to Judaism, was a Roman ally with such a passion for building that extensive remains of his grand building schemes can be seen to this day. It was he who built Caesarea with such opulence that the Romans later used it as their capital. In Jerusalem he constructed the Antonia Fortress at the northwest corner of the Temple area so the Roman troops could be nearby, as Josephus put it, to "watch for any sign of popular discontent." He reconstructed the Temple, following the original ground plan, but he doubled the height of its golden facade and extended its porch. He also covered the Temple Mount with a large platform supported by retaining walls. A section of the western wall, now generally known by Christians as the Wailing Wall, has been revered by Jews for the past 1900 years as their most sacred holy place. The Inner Temple was surrounded by an outer court or the Court of Gentiles, which again was enclosed by massive walls encompassing the entire Temple area. The Eastern Gate led to the Women's Court of the Inner Temple,

Jerusalem: Model of the Herodian Temple and first-century Jerusalem, on display at the Holyland Hotel (Acts 21:27-40)

Istanbul: Inscription, now in the Archeological Museum, prohibiting Gentiles from entering the Temple (Acts 21:28). Translation: "Let no one of foreign race proceed within the railing of the precinct in the temple. If anyone is caught, he shall be liable unto himself for his subsequent death."

so called because women were not allowed to proceed further. In each of its four corners were chambers. Two of these chambers were used for storing wood and oil, one was used for the purification of lepers, and the fourth was used by the Nazarites. This court also seems to have contained the treasury (Mark 12:41; Luke 21:1). (When St. Paul was seized he was dragged out of the Women's Court down the flight of stairs into the Outer Court. The gates shut behind him must have been the Eastern Gate which, according to Josephus, required the force of twenty men to close.) From the Nicanor

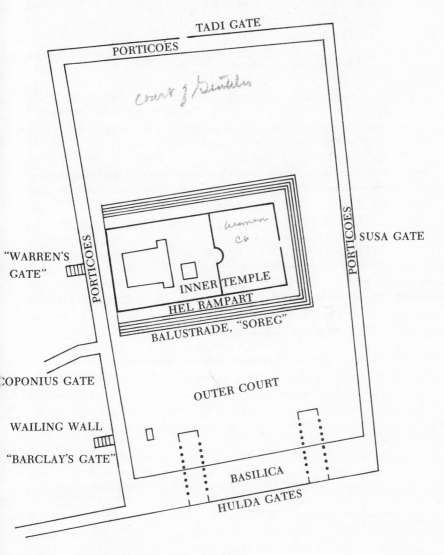

TADI GATE

PORTICOES

court of Gentiles

"WARREN'S GATE"

PORTICOES

PORTICOES

SUSA GATE

Women Ct.

INNER TEMPLE

HEL RAMPART

BALUSTRADE, "SOREG"

COPONIUS GATE

OUTER COURT

WAILING WALL

"BARCLAY'S GATE"

BASILICA

HULDA GATES

Jerusalem: Plan of the Temple mount

Gate a flight of fifteen semicircular steps led from the Women's Court to the Court of Israel, which was separated from the Court of the Priests by a low balustrade. In the Court of the Priests were the great altar and the slaughtering area, with its marble tables, posts, and hooks, since "without the shedding of blood there is no forgiveness of sins" (Heb. 9:22).

The sanctuary was divided into the Porch, the Holy Place, and the Holy of Holies. The Porch, wider than the rest of the sanctuary, was separated by a richly embroidered veil from the Holy Place, where the Table of the Shewbread stood, and on it the Menorah, the seven branched candlestick. The Holy of Holies was behind the Holy Place, separated from it by another veil. In Herod's time the Holy of Holies was empty, although it once had housed the golden Altar of Incense, the gold covered Ark of the Covenant, and the Tablets of the Covenant (Heb. 9:2-5).

The rumor that the sanctuary had been profaned caused a violent riot. St. Paul was seized by the mob, and the Levites, the guardians of the Holy of Holies, quickly closed the Eastern Gate to prevent the pollution of the sanctuary by a possible murder. The commotion in the Temple area was seen by the guards stationed in the Antonia Fortress, who immediately notified Claudius Lysias, the tribune of the cohort (commander of the garrison), that "all Jerusalem was in confusion" (Acts 21:31). Lysias led some of his men into the Temple Court and took custody of the Apostle as the mob was beating him, thereby saving his life. St. Paul was bound by two chains, for Lysias suspected him to be the Egyptian rebel who, according to Josephus, had stirred up a revolt during the procuratorship of Felix and had led 4,000 (Josephus says 30,000) Assassins — not into — but out of the wilderness to the Mount of Olives. The mob made immediate interrogation impossible, for "some in the crowd shouted one thing, some another" (Acts 21:34), so Lysias had St. Paul taken towards

Jerusalem: Plan of the Temple

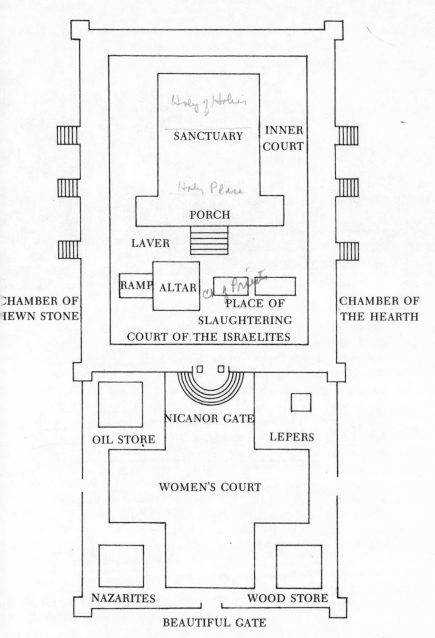

SANCTUARY

INNER COURT

Holy of Holies

Holy Place

PORCH

LAVER

RAMP ALTAR

PLACE OF SLAUGHTERING

CHAMBER OF HEWN STONE

CHAMBER OF THE HEARTH

COURT OF THE ISRAELITES

NICANOR GATE

OIL STORE

LEPERS

WOMEN'S COURT

NAZARITES

WOOD STORE

BEAUTIFUL GATE

31

Jerusalem: The Antonia Fortress (Acts 21:34)

the barracks of the fortress. Before reaching the fortress, however, St. Paul spoke to the commanding officer, who was startled to hear his prisoner speak Greek and was therefore not the Egyptian rebel. When he also learned that St. Paul was a Jew from Tarsus he permitted the Apostle to speak to the people. St. Paul stood on the steps leading from the Temple area to the Antonia Fortress and addressed the people, probably in Aramaic, which St. Luke calls Hebrew.

In the northwest corner of the Haram ash-Sharif at the base of the minaret (the Manarat al-Ghawanima, named after Shaikh Ghanim al-Ali, who died in Damascus in 1167) are traces of steps cut in the rock. These stairs leading to the Antonia Fortress probably are on the same site as those on which St. Paul stood when he addressed the Jews in the Temple area. Repairs carried out in the late 1950's removed most of the old stairway and replaced it with a new one.

Jerusalem: Stairs leading to the Antonia Fortress (Acts 21:40)

St. Paul's Defense

aramaic

And when they heard that he addressed them in the Hebrew language, they were the more quiet. And he said:

"I am a Jew, born at Tarsus in Cilicia, but brought up in this city at the feet of Gamaliel, educated according to the strict manner of the law of our fathers, being zealous for God as you all are this day. I persecuted this Way to the death, binding and delivering to prison both men and women, as the high priest and the whole council of elders bear me witness. From them I received letters to the brethren, and I journeyed to Damascus to take those also who were there and bring them in bonds to Jerusalem to be punished.

"As I made my journey and drew near to Damascus, about noon a great light from heaven suddenly shone about me. And I fell to the ground and heard a voice saying to me, 'Saul, Saul, why do you persecute me?' And I answered, 'Who are you, Lord?' And he said to me, 'I am Jesus of Nazareth whom you are persecuting.' Now those who were with me saw the light but did not hear the voice of the one who was speaking to me. And I said, 'What shall I do, Lord?' And the Lord said to me, 'Rise, and go into Damascus, and there you will be told all that is appointed for you to do.' And when I could not see because of the brightness of that light, I was led by the hand by those who were with me, and came into Damascus.

"And one Ananias, a devout man according to the law, well spoken of by all the Jews who lived there, came to me, and standing by me said to me, 'Brother Saul, receive your sight.' And in that very hour I received my sight and saw him. And he said, 'The God of our fathers appointed you to know his will, to see the Just One and to hear a voice from his mouth; for you will be a witness for him to all men of what you have seen and heard. And now why do you wait? Rise and be baptized, and wash away your sins, calling on his name.'

"When I had returned to Jerusalem and was praying in the temple, I fell into a trance and saw him saying to me, 'Make haste and get quickly out of Jerusalem, because they will not accept your testimony about me.' And I said, 'Lord, they themselves know that in every synagogue I imprisoned and beat those who believed in thee. And when the blood of Stephen thy witness was shed, I also was standing by and approving, and keeping the garments of those who killed him.' And he said to me, 'Depart, for I will send you far away to the Gentiles.'"

Acts 22:2-21

This speech is St. Luke's second account of the Apostle's conversion on the Damascus Road, which he also recorded in chapter 9:1-19. The importance of the Damascus Road experience for the Apostle — to which St. Paul repeatedly referred in his letters (Gal. 1:15-16; I Cor. 9:1, 15:8, II Cor. 4:6) — cannot be exaggerated, for it provided him with the distinct assurance of apostolic authenticity. St. Luke emphasizes that St. Paul was the divinely appointed Apostle to the Gentiles in three narratives: Acts 9:1-31; 22:6-21; 26:12-18. In the first account, probably an early Antiochene tradition, no definite call is addressed to St. Paul directly. As he neared Damascus a heavenly light suddenly flashed about him. (Tradition has preserved this site, approximately 17 km. southwest of Damascus near the road to Qunaitra. It is now commemorated by the Greek Orthodox Church of the Conversion of St. Paul. The cornerstone of the modern church was laid in 1956 by His Holiness Alexis, Patriarch of Moscow and All Russia.)

The Apostle, blinded for three days (Acts 9:9), remained in the house of Judas on the Vicus Rectus or the Street Called Straight. (Today this street, known as Suq at-Tawil or the Long Bazaar, is lined with shops selling brass, carpets,

Damascus: Greek Orthodox Church of the Conversion of St. Paul (Acts 22:6)

Damascene brocade, and furniture inlaid with ivory and mother-of-pearl.) While he was there, Ananias, a Damascene, was instructed by the Lord to find St. Paul so that he might regain his sight. St. Paul's sight returned as soon as Ananias touched him, and Paul was baptized immediately afterwards. (According to a medieval tradition the house of Ananias was just off the Street Called Straight, on what is

Damascus: Entrance to the street called Straight, near the site of the house of Ananias (Acts 9:10-19, 22:12-16)

Damascus: Terra Santa Cross sign above the entrance to the house of Ananias (Acts 9:10-19, 22:12-16)

now called Dshafar Street. On the traditional site the subterranean Franciscan chapel of St. Ananias, recently reconstructed, has remains of a Roman temple and a basilica.) In the first account of Paul's conversion, the role he was to play was stated by the Lord: "Go, for he is a chosen instrument of mine to carry my name before the Gentiles and kings and the sons of Israel" (Acts 9:15).

This account ends with St. Paul's ministry to the Jews in Damascus, which was so successful that many Jews plotted to kill him, watching the gates so they could attack him when he left the city. "But his disciples took him by night and let him down over the wall, lowering him in a basket" (Acts 9:25). (The Apostle's escape from the city is commemorated by the Greek Catholic Church of St. Paul in the Walls. This church, dedicated on June 29, 1941, was built on the site of a former sanctuary at Bab Kisan, of which, however, only a single column has survived.)

It makes little difference precisely how the Apostle received the divine commission to turn to the Gentiles. St.

Paul was certain of his task, and this he wanted his accusers to understand. He postponed, however, mentioning the Gentiles until the end of his speech, for he must have known the outburst of indignation it would provoke. For the assembled Jews in the Temple Court, the thought of uncircumcised pagans enjoying the same spiritual opportunities as the sons of Abraham was blasphemy.

Up to this word they listened to him; then they lifted up their voices and said, "Away with such a fellow from the earth! For he ought not to live." And as they cried out and waved their garments and threw dust into the

Damascus: Greek Catholic Church of St. Paul in the Walls (Acts 9:25)

air, the tribune commanded him to be brought into the barracks, and ordered him to be examined by scourging, to find out why they shouted thus against him. But when they had tied him up with the thongs, Paul said to the centurion who was standing by. "Is it lawful for you to scourge a man who is a Roman citizen, and uncondemned?" When the centurion heard that, he went to the tribune and said to him, "What are you about to do? For this man is a Roman citizen." So the tribune came and said to him, "Tell me, are you a Roman citizen?" And he said, "Yes." The tribune answered, "I bought this citizenship for a large sum." Paul said, "But I was born a citizen." So those who were about to examine him withdrew from him instantly; and the tribune also was afraid, for he realized that Paul was a Roman citizen and that he had bound him.

Acts 22:22-29

St. Paul's reference to the Gentiles led to the second outburst by the mob, this time openly demanding even his death. Lysias did not know Aramaic and could not understand this new outburst, so he ordered St. Paul to be taken immediately into the barracks to be whipped until he confessed his crime. Being whipped was not a new experience for St. Paul. Five times the Jews had given him forty lashes less one, and three times, once at Philippi (Acts 16:22-23), he had been beaten (II Cor. 11:23-25).

As he had done in Philippi several years before (Acts 16:37), so here in the Roman barracks in Jerusalem St. Paul claimed his rights as a Roman citizen. And again Cicero's statement applied: "How often has this exclamation *civis Romanus sum* brought help and safety even among barbarians in the remotest parts of the earth." The claim of Roman citizenship produced immediate effect. The centurion told Claudius Lysias, who quickly verified the Apostle's citizenship. Claudius Lysias had purchased his citizenship for "a large sum," probably during the reign of

Claudius, as it was common for new citizens to adopt the name of the reigning emperor. Dio Cassius reports that "Inasmuch as practically everywhere Romans were esteemed above foreigners, many sought the franchise by personal application to the emperor and many bought it from Messalina and the Caesarians. For this reason, though the right was at first bartered only for great sums, it later was cheapened by the facility with which it could be obtained..." St. Paul, however, had inherited his citizenship from his parents. A 4th century tradition recorded by St. Jerome states that St. Paul's parents were carried away from Gischala, the modern village of Qush Halav in northern Israel, to Tarsus, when the whole province was laid waste by the Romans and the Jews were scattered. It is likely that St. Paul's parents were given Roman citizenship while in Palestine, probably in return for services rendered to Mark Antony.

St. Paul Before the Sanhedrin

But on the morrow, desiring to know the real reason why the Jews accused him, he unbound him, and commanded the chief priests and all the council to meet, and he brought Paul down and set him before them.

And Paul, looking intently at the council, said, "Brethren, I have lived before God in all good conscience up to this day." And the high priest Ananias commanded those who stood by him to strike him on the mouth. Then Paul said to him, "God shall strike you, you whitewashed wall! Are you sitting to judge me according to the law, and yet contrary to the law you order me to be struck?" Those who stood by said, "Would you revile God's high priest?" And Paul said, "I did not know, brethren, that he was the high priest; for it is written, 'You shall not speak evil of a ruler of your people.'"

41

But when Paul perceived that one part were Sadducees and the other Pharisees, he cried out in the council, "Brethren, I am a Pharisee, a son of Pharisees; with respect to the hope and the resurrection of the dead I am on trial." And when he had said this, a dissension arose between the Pharisees and the Sadducees; and the assembly was divided. For the Sadducees say that there is no resurrection, nor angel, nor spirit; but the Pharisees acknowledge them all. Then a great clamor arose; and some of the scribes of the Pharisees' party stood up and contended, "We find nothing wrong in this man. What if a spirit or an angel spoke to him?" And when the dissension became violent, the tribune, afraid that Paul would be torn in pieces by them, commanded the soldiers to go down and take him by force from among them and bring him into the barracks.

Acts 22:30-23:10

Afraid that he had exceeded his authority, but ignorant of the real causes of the upheaval, Lysias summoned the Sanhedrin with the high priest and brought the Apostle before them. (The chamber of the Sanhedrin where St. Paul defended himself was on the western side of the Temple area, north of the Wailing Wall, on the site of the Madrasa at-Tankiziya, also called the *mahkameh* or Tribunal, because during the Ottoman period it served as a law court.) Addressing the council must have been a strange experience for St. Paul. Some of the members could well have been his fellow students when he studied at the feet of Gamaliel. Ananias had been appointed high priest by Herod Agrippa II in 48 and, according to Josephus, he was a Sadducee well known for his temper and insolence. St. Paul began his address by saying, "Brethren, I have lived before God in all

Jerusalem: Probable site of the Chamber of the Sanhedrin, now "Home of the Perfect Quran" (Acts 22:30)

good conscience up to this day" (Acts 23:1). But before he had finished, Ananias ordered him to be struck on the mouth, angering St. Paul to the point of calling the wrath of God upon the high priest. If this was a prophetic denunciation, it was fulfilled a few years later when Ananias was murdered by the Assassins, the *Sicarii,* in the Jewish War. St. Paul's calling Ananias a "whitewashed wall" may refer to our Lord's denunciation of the scribes and Pharisees, whom He compared to whitewashed tombs (Matt. 23:27).

St. Paul knew the composition and workings of the Sanhedrin well. Although he may not actually have been a member of the council when Stephen was judged, he had taken part in the dispute as a member of the Cilician synagogue and had given his consent to the execution (Acts 8:1). He knew of the importance of the high priestly office, and either with humility or calm irony he replied that he had not realized that it was the high priest who had ordered him struck. At the same time he quoted the Mosaic Law that prohibited speaking ill of a ruler of the people (Ex. 22:28). He also knew that the Sanhedrin was composed of the high priest's party, the Sadducees, and some Pharisees who, however united they might outwardly appear, were deeply divided in their religious faith. When he, therefore, cried out in the council, "I am a Pharisee, a son of Pharisees; with respect to the hope and the resurrection of the dead I am on trial" (Acts 23:6), he knew that the council would dissolve in chaos. The Pharisees rallied to the Apostle's defense against the Sadducees, and the chamber of the Sanhedrin became the scene of violent dissension. Claudius Lysias, fearful for the life of a Roman citizen, sent soldiers to rescue St. Paul a second time.

ST. PAUL IN CHAINS IN CAESAREA

St. Paul's Transfer to Caesarea

The following night the Lord stood by him and said, "Take courage, for as you have testified about me at Jerusalem, so you must bear witness also at Rome."

When it was day, the Jews made a plot and bound themselves by an oath neither to eat nor to drink till they had killed Paul. There were more than forty who made this conspiracy. And they went to the chief priests and elders, and said, "We have strictly bound ourselves by an oath to taste no food till we have killed Paul. You therefore, along with the council, give notice now to the tribune to bring him down to you, as though you were going to determine his case more exactly. And we are ready to kill him before he comes near."

Now the son of Paul's sister heard of their ambush; so he went and entered the barracks and told Paul. And Paul called one of the centurions and said, "Bring this young man to the tribune; for he has something to tell him." So he took him and brought him to the tribune and said, "Paul the prisoner called me and asked me to bring this young man to you, as he has something to say to you." The tribune took him by the hand, and going aside asked him privately, "What is it that you have to tell me?" And he said, "The Jews have agreed to ask you to bring Paul down to the council tomorrow, as though they were going to inquire somewhat more closely about him. But do not yield to them; for more than forty of their men lie in ambush for him, having bound themselves by an oath neither to eat nor drink till they have killed him; and now they are ready, waiting for the promise from you." So the tribune dismissed the young man, charging him, "Tell no one that you have informed me of this."

Then he called two of the centurions and said, "At the third hour of the night get ready two hundred soldiers with seventy horsemen and two hundred spearmen to go as far as Caesarea. Also provide mounts for Paul to ride, and bring him safely to Felix the governor." And he wrote a letter to this effect:

"Claudius Lysias to His Excellency the governor Felix, greeting. This man was seized by the Jews, and was about to be killed by them, when I came upon them with the soldiers and rescued him, having learned that he was a Roman citizen. And desiring to know the charge on which they accused him, I brought him down to their council. I found that he was accused about questions of their law, but charged with nothing deserving death or imprisonment. And when it was disclosed to me that there would be a plot against the man, I sent him to you at once, ordering his accusers also to state before you what they have against him."

So the soldiers, according to their instructions, took Paul and brought him by night to Antipatris. And on the morrow they returned to the barracks, leaving the horsemen to go on with him. When they came to Caesarea and delivered the letter to the governor, they presented Paul also before him. On reading the letter, he asked to what province he belonged. When he learned that he was from Cilicia he said, "I will hear you when your accusers arrive." And he commanded him to be guarded in Herod's praetorium.

Acts 23:11-35

During the night, while being held in the Roman barracks in the Antonia Fortress, St. Paul again was strengthened by a vision of the Lord. The last time he had had such an experience was when the Corinthian Jews were threatening him. While staying in the house of Priscilla and Aquila St. Paul saw the Lord Who spoke to him with the words: "Do not be afraid, but speak and do not be silent; for I am with you, and no man shall attack you to harm you; for I have many people in this city" (Acts 18:9-10). Now the Lord encouraged him again, pointing out that he must witness also in Rome. The Apostle had planned to go to Rome ever since he had written the Roman Christians from Corinth. Now, in Jerusalem, the prospects appeared dim, but the vision confirmed that he would attain his goal.

The morning after St. Paul's arrest more than forty fanatics swore neither to eat nor drink until they had murdered the Apostle. They demanded that the Sanhedrin call St. Paul to appear again before the council. The conspirators intended to kill him after he left the Antonia Fortress for the meeting. The plot would have succeeded had it not been for one of St. Paul's nephews, the son of his sister. This sister may have been married to one of the forty fanatics and may have sent her son to the barracks to warn her brother. St. Paul called one of the centurions and requested him to take his nephew to Claudius Lysias, who received him kindly. The youth explained the plot, ending by saying that the conspirators were waiting only for Lysias to permit St. Paul to appear before the proposed meeting of the Sanhedrin. After Lysias had heard the young man he summoned two of his centurions and ordered them to assemble 200 infantry, 70 cavalry, and 200 spearmen to be ready at 9 P.M. to escort the Apostle to Felix, the governor (procurator) of Judaea, in Caesarea. Since this was a long journey, he gave directions that more than one horse should be provided for the prisoner. The size of the force was large because Lysias knew that at least 40 men had sworn to kill the Apostle and he may have feared more disturbances. Lysias wrote to Felix briefly explaining the affair, including that he thought there was no breach of Roman law in the charges made against St. Paul by his countrymen, and that he had ordered St. Paul's accusers to appear before the Roman procurator.

The troops escorting St. Paul traveled during the night to the new settlement of Antipatris, about two thirds of the way to Caesarea. Antipatris, built by Herod the Great and named in memory of his father Antipater, was constructed on the

ruins of Aphek, a strategically important city on the main north - south highway along the coastal plain, at the junction of the road leading to Shiloh. At Aphek the Israelites had fought one of their major battles against the Philistines during the days of Samuel (I Sam. 4).

After spending the rest of the night in Antipatris the infantry returned to Jerusalem, for they were no longer needed. While in Antipatris St. Paul would have remembered that here, according to Hebrew tradition, Simon the high priest and the Jewish elders from Jerusalem had greeted Alexander the Great on his way to Egypt. After sleeping at the Roman post St. Paul and his escort continued to Caesarea, where the officer in charge promptly delivered both Lysias's letter and the prisoner to the Roman governor. After learning from what province St. Paul came, Felix dismissed the Apostle and ordered that he be accommodated in the praetorium, the palace built by Herod the Great when he reconstructed the city.

St. Paul and Felix

And after five days the high priest Ananias came down with some elders and a spokesman, one Tertullus. They laid before the governor their case against Paul; and when he was called, Tertullus began to accuse him, saying:

"Since through you we enjoy much peace, and since by your provision, most excellent Felix, reforms are introduced on behalf of this nation, in every way and everywhere we accept this with all gratitude. But, to detain you no further, I beg you in your kindness to hear

Caesarea: The ruins of Herod's palace (Acts 23:33-35)

us briefly. For we have found this man a pestilent fellow, an agitator among all the Jews throughout the world, and a ringleader of the sect of the Nazarenes. He even tried to profane the temple, but we seized him. By examining him yourself you will be able to learn from him about everything of which we accuse him."

The Jews also joined in the charge, affirming that all this was so.

And when the governor had motioned to him to speak, Paul replied:

"Realizing that for many years you have been judge over this nation, I cheerfully make my defense. As you may ascertain, it is not more than twelve days since I went up to worship at Jerusalem; and they did not find me disputing with any one or stirring up a crowd, either in the temple or in the synagogues, or in the city. Neither can they prove to you what they now bring up against me. But this I admit to you, that according to the Way, which they call a sect, I worship the God of our fathers, believing everything laid down by the law or written in the prophets, having a hope in God which these themselves accept, that there will be a resurrection of both the just and the unjust. So I always take pains to have a clear conscience toward God and toward men. Now after some years I came to bring my nation alms and offerings. As I was doing this, they found me purified in the temple, without any crowd or tumult. But some Jews from Asia — they ought to be here before you and to make an accusation, if they have anything against me. Or else let these men themselves say what wrongdoing they found when I stood before the council, except this one thing which I cried out while standing among them. 'With respect to the resurrection of the dead I am on trial before you this day.' "

But Felix having a rather accurate knowledge of the Way, put them off, saying, "When Lysias the tribune comes down, I will decide your case." Then he gave orders to the centurion that he should be kept in custody but should have some liberty, and that none of his friends should be prevented from attending to his needs.

After some days Felix came with his wife Drusilla who was a Jewess; and he sent for Paul and heard him speak upon faith in Christ Jesus. And as he argued about justice and self-control and future judgement, Felix was alarmed and said, "Go away for the present; when I have an opportunity I will summon you." At the same time he hoped that money would be given him by Paul. So he sent for him often and conversed with him. But when two years had elapsed, Felix was succeeded by Porcius Festus; and desiring to do the Jews a favor, Felix left Paul in prison.

Acts 24:1-27

At the time of St. Paul's last visit to Jerusalem and Judaea, the country was ruled by Herod Agrippa II, a Hellenized Jew who had been given the title of king by the Romans, as had his father before him. Although also a Roman favorite, Agrippa II did not inherit his father's kingdom, but only the tetrachies of Philip and Lysias to which some towns in Galilee and Perea later were added. During his rule — in the sixties of the 1st century — the Jews revolted, but were harshly suppressed by the Romans. Agrippa had tried to prevent his countrymen from rebelling, and when war broke out he sided with the Romans. He had been raised in Rome and he remained loyal to Rome. He witnessed the destruction of Jerusalem in 70 and lived until the end of the 1st century.

Herod Agrippa II's two sisters, the younger Drusilla (Acts 24:24) and the elder Bernice (Acts 25:13, 23; 26:30), appear in accounts of contemporary historians as well as in St. Luke's story. According to Josephus, Felix enticed Drusilla from her husband Aziz, King of Emesa, with the assistance of the Cypriot magician Atomus or Etoimas. This man might have been the sorcerer at the court of Sergius Paulus in Paphos, for the Western Text of the Bible calls Sergius Paulus's sorcerer

Etoimas rather than Elymas (Acts 13:8). Tacitus incorrectly refers to Drusilla as the granddaughter of Antony and Cleopatra. Drusilla and her child by Felix died in the eruption of Vesuvius. Bernice, the elder sister of Drusilla, was married to her uncle Herod, King of Chalcis, and after his death, according to Josephus and Juvenal, lived with her brother Herod Agrippa II as his mistress. For a while she was married to Polemo, King of Cilicia, but she left him and returned to her brother. Later she became an admirer of Vespasian, and her carnal relations with Vespasian's son are mentioned by the historians Suetonius and Tacitus. According to Dio Cassius the emperor Titus seems to have been saved from marrying this immoral princess only by the indignation of the Romans; but she became his mistress nevertheless. On one occasion, however, she showed compassion for her own Jewish people by appearing as a barefooted suppliant to intercede for the Jews before the brutal Roman governor Gessius Florus. On this occasion "they actually would have killed her if she had not escaped in time into the royal palace."

The governor of Judaea was Antonius Felix, who had been appointed by the emperor Claudius. He was named Antonius Felix because he was a freedman of Claudius's mother, Antonia. Tacitus reports that Antonius Felix was efficient in that he had freed the country from the threat of robbers, had driven away the Egyptian fanatic with whom Claudius Lysias had identified St. Paul (Acts 21:38), and had quelled the civil strife between Jews and Greeks in Caesarea. At the same time, however, Tacitus records that Antonius Felix "practised every kind of cruelty and lust, wielding the power of a king with all the instincts of a slave." He was responsible for the assassination in the Temple sanctuary of Jonathan the high priest, who had helped Antonius Felix get appointed as governor.

Five days after St. Paul's arrival in Caesarea the high priest Ananias, the elders, and Tertullus, a Roman advocate for the prosecution, appeared before the governor. Tertullus would have addressed the procurator in Latin, which is supported by the typical Latin judicial character of the speech. After the customary opening phrases of praise he accused St. Paul of causing disturbances "among all the Jews throughout the world," of being "a ringleader of the sect of the Nazarenes," and of attempting "to profane the Temple" (Acts 24:5 - 6). The third accusation was the most serious, for it was not only an offense against Jewish, but also against Roman law (Acts 21:28). The Western Text of the Bible adds that Claudius Lysias, the commandant of the garrison in Jerusalem, had forcibly removed St. Paul just as the Sanhedrin was about to judge him by religious law. The Jews believed the Apostle ought to have been their prisoner who, by defiling the Temple, deserved death. In their eyes Lysias had intervened unjustly in their legal proceedings.

St. Paul opened his defense by tactfully acknowledging Felix's many years of experience of legal proceedings. Then he refuted each of Tertullus's charges, stating that since his recent arrival in Jerusalem he had caused no disturbances in the city, that he had never forsaken the Law and the Prophets and that, far from profaning the Temple, he had been in the Temple observing the laws of the ritual without any crowd or tumult. Moreover, he pointed out that the accusations against him were made by Asian Jews who should have been present to accuse him.

Felix did not wish to judge this sensitive political issue alone, so he deferred the inquiry until Claudius Lysias could come down from Jerusalem. The governor had lived in Caesarea for several years and must have come in touch with "the Way," one of the earliest names used by the Christian community. (It is used in the Acts of the Apostles six times: 9:2; 19:9, 23; 22:4; 24:14, 22). Felix, furthermore, may have been instructed about the people of "the Way" by his Jewish wife, Drusilla.

Meanwhile, the Apostle was held in custody, although his friends were permitted to attend to his needs. St. Luke is silent about any visit by Claudius Lysias to Caesarea or about any judicial proceedings, so Felix may have mentioned Lysias during the hearing only as a delaying tactic. A few days later

Felix and his wife Drusilla decided to hear St. Paul, and the Apostle saw this as his opportunity to preach to them Jesus Christ. As he spoke "about justice and self-control and the future judgement" Felix became alarmed. It is not surprising, considering the corrupt administration and the self indulgent character of the governor, that he preferred to interrupt St. Paul's discourse, but he did not release the Apostle. Instead, Felix followed a well known practice by keeping the prisoner, expecting "that money would be given him by Paul" (Acts 24:26). Josephus records that Albinus, who succeeded Porcius Festus as governor of Judaea, released many prisoners, but only those from whom he received a bribe. Felix knew that the Christians helped each other in need, and he may have hoped that other believers would pay for the Apostle's release. He often sent for St. Paul and conversed with him, presumably to give the Apostle opportunities to buy his freedom, but Felix's hope remained unfulfilled. St. Paul remained in the praetorium until Felix was removed from office in 61.

Although St. Luke does not name any of St. Paul's visitors, one of them probably would have been Philip the Evangelist, whose hospitality in Caesarea St. Paul had enjoyed for many days when he arrived in Palestine (Acts 21:8). St. Paul may have met with Philip, who represented the Caesarean church, to discuss a letter to the Jewish section of the Jerusalem congregation to reconcile the extreme legalistic and the more liberal parties within the church. Divergent views had alienated certain leaders from some of the congregation. The Apostle may have discussed these divisions with Philip, who then may have written the Letter to the Hebrews, which St. Paul concluded with a few personal remarks.

There are several theories regarding the authorship, place of writing, and destination of the Letter to the Hebrews, about the author of which the New Testament gives no information. If the author knew Hebrew, he preferred to use the Septuagint Greek version of the Jewish Scriptures. The Alexandrian Fathers considered St. Paul the author, Tertullian suggested St. Barnabas, Martin Luther suggested Apollos, and others have considered the author Aquila, Priscilla, Silas, or Timothy. The Western Church did not accept this letter as Paul's or even as Holy Scripture until the middle of the 4th century.

The recipients of the Letter to the Hebrews had been Christians for some time, for the writer admonished them: "For though by this time you ought to be teachers, you need some one to teach you again the first principles of God's word" (Heb. 5:12). Moreover, this letter was not addressed to a church but to some members of a congregation, for they are asked to greet their "leaders and all the saints" (Heb. 13:24). The greetings from "those who come from Italy" may be Jewish Christian pilgrims passing through Caesarea on their way to attend the Passover celebrations in Jerusalem. They also could have been soldier converts — like the centurion Cornelius of the Italian cohort (Acts 10:1) — members of the *Cohors II Italica Civium Romanorum* stationed in Caesarea, who sent their greetings.

We may never learn the author, place of writing, and destination of this letter, and unless we do, we must share the opinion of Origen of Alexandria that "God alone knows who wrote this epistle." Nonetheless, a Caesarean origin and a Jerusalem destination remain possible.

Caesarea: Drawing of thirteenth-century Crusader seal showing St. Peter baptizing Cornelius (Acts 10:48)

St. Paul and Festus

Now when Festus had come into his province, after three days he went up to Jerusalem from Caesarea. And the chief priests and the principal men of the Jews informed him against Paul; and they urged him, asking as a favor to have the man sent to Jerusalem, planning an ambush to kill him on the way. Festus replied that Paul was being kept at Caesarea, and that he himself intended to go there shortly. "So," he said, "let the men of authority among you go down with me, and if there is anything wrong about the man, let them accuse him."

When he had stayed among them not more than eight or ten days, he went down to Caesarea, and the next day he took his seat on the tribunal and ordered Paul to be brought. And when he had come, the Jews who had gone down from Jerusalem stood about him, bringing against him many serious charges which they could not prove. Paul said in his defense, "Neither against the law of the Jews, nor against the temple, nor against Caesar have I offended at all." But Festus, wishing to do the Jews a favor, said to Paul, "Do you wish to go up to Jerusalem and there be tried on these charges before me?" But Paul said, "I am standing before Caesar's tribunal, where I ought to be tried; to the Jews I have done no wrong, as you know very well. If then I am a wrongdoer, and have committed anything for which I deserve to die, I do not seek to escape death; but if there is nothing in their charges against me, no one can give me up to them. I appeal to Caesar." Then Festus, when he had conferred with his council, answered, "You have appealed to Caesar; to Caesar you shall go."

Now when some days had passed, Agrippa the king and Bernice arrived at Caesarea to welcome Festus. And as they stayed there many days, Festus laid Paul's case before the king, saying, "There is a man left prisoner by Felix; and when I was at Jerusalem, the chief priests and the elders of the Jews gave information about him, asking for sentence against him. I answered them that it was not the custom of the Romans to give up any one before the accused met the accusers face to face, and had opportunity to make his defense concerning the charge laid against him. When therefore they came together here, I made no delay, but on the next day took my seat on the tribunal and ordered the man to be brought in. When the accusers stood up, they brought no charge in his case of such evils as I supposed; but they had certain points of dispute with him about their own superstition and about one Jesus, who was dead, but whom Paul asserted to be alive. Being at a loss how to investigate these questions, I asked whether he wished to go to Jerusalem and be tried there regarding them. But when Paul had appealed to be kept in custody for the decision of the emperor, I commanded him to be held until I could send him to Caesar."

And Agrippa said to Festus, "I should like to hear the man myself." "Tomorrow," said he, "you shall hear him."

So on the morrow Agrippa and Bernice came with great pomp, and they entered the audience hall with the military tribunes and the prominent men of the city. Then by command of Festus Paul was brought in. And Festus said, "King Agrippa and all who are present with us, you see this man about whom the whole Jewish people petitioned me, both at Jerusalem and here, shouting that he ought not to live any longer. But I found that he had done nothing deserving death; and as he himself appealed to the emperor, I decided to send him. But I have nothing definite to write to my lord about him. Therefore I have brought him before you, and especially before you, King Agrippa, that, after we have examined him, I may have something to write. For it seems to me unreasonable, in sending a prisoner, not to indicate the charges against him."

Acts 25:1-27

The governor Porcius Festus, who succeeded Felix, probably arrived in Caesarea in the summer of 61. In his *Antiquities* Josephus devoted several paragraphs to Festus's administration in which the new governor is depicted as an honorable man. He suppressed the Assassins or *Sicarii* who still interrupted the peace and security of the province. During much of the period of his office, which probably lasted only one year, he was engaged in a dispute with the Jerusalem elders about the rebuilding of the Temple wall, which would have prevented the Roman guards from watching the activities within the Temple area.

Three days after arriving in his province, Festus went from Caesarea up to Jerusalem where he was promptly presented with charges against St. Paul. The chief priests and the leading men among the Jews asked that St. Paul be brought to Jerusalem to be tried again before the Sanhedrin; in fact, they planned to murder him on the way. The peace of which Tertullus had spoken (Acts 24:2) was not holding and assassinations by the *Sicarii* were a common experience. One more murder would not excite particular official attention. Festus refused, however, and said that the accusers could travel to Caesarea to face the accused.

The day after Festus returned to Caesarea he took his seat on the tribunal, thereby, as the emperor's representative, safeguarding St. Paul's rights as a Roman citizen. Presumably, the charges brought by the members of the Sanhedrin against the Apostle were the same as those Tertullus had listed when he addressed Felix (Acts 24:5-6), for in his defense the Apostle said: "Neither against the law of the Jews (heresy), nor against the Temple (sacrilege), nor against Caesar (treason) have I offended at all" (Acts 25:8). Festus, probably tired of the whole case, tried to compromise, realizing that in the eyes of the accusers the offence was religious rather than political. Unsure how to deal with the matter and wishing to do the Jews a favor, he suggested to St. Paul to go up to Jerusalem and be tried there, presumably by the Sanhedrin, in Felix's presence. But the Apostle knew of the danger of this proposal and, while protesting against

58

being handed over to the jurisdiction of the Sanhedrin, he called upon his rights as a Roman citizen and said, "I appeal to Caesar." Roman law did not require a written appeal to be lodged and the simple statement of appeal to Caesar suspended the proceedings.

Festus probably was surprised by St. Paul's move, and he conferred with his advisors. In some cases the right of appeal was not permitted; bandits and pirates, for example, could be executed by the governor notwithstanding their appeal to the emperor. In the case of St. Paul, however, there was no doubt. "You have appealed to Caesar; to Caesar you shall go" (Acts 25:12).

A few days later Herod Agrippa II, with his sister-mistress Bernice, arrived in Caesarea on a courtesy visit to the new governor. Agrippa II was well acquainted with Jewish law for he was in charge of the Temple treasures and appointed the high priest. Festus sought his advice. He recounted to the king the events leading to the Apostle's appeal to Caesar, admitting his own ignorance about the dispute which dealt with the "one Jesus, who was dead, but whom Paul asserted to be alive" (Acts 25:19).

Festus's opinion of the situation is described in greater detail in the Western Text of the Bible, which reads as follows:

> The whole Jewish people petitioned me, both in Jerusalem and here, that I should hand him over to them for torture without defense. But I was not able to hand him over on account of instructions which we have from the emperor. So I said that if anyone wished to accuse him he should follow me to Caesarea where he was in custody. And when they arrived they clamoured that his life should be taken away. But when I heard this and that side, I found that in no respect was he worthy of death. But when I said, do you wish to be tried with them in Jerusalem? he appealed to Caesar.

St. Paul Before Agrippa

Agrippa said to Paul, "You have permission to speak for yourself." Then Paul stretched out his hand and made his defense:

"I think myself fortunate that it is before you, King Agrippa, I am to make my defense today against all the accusations of the Jews, because you are especially familiar with all customs and controversies of the Jews; therefore I beg you to listen to me patiently.

"My manner of life from my youth, spent from the beginning among my own nation and at Jerusalem, is known by all the Jews. They have known for a long time, if they are willing to testify, that according to the strictest party of our religion I have lived as a Pharisee. And now I stand here on trial for hope in the promise made by God to our fathers, to which our twelve tribes hope to attain, as they earnestly worship night and day. And for this hope I am accused by Jews, O king! Why is it thought incredible by any of you that God raises the dead?

"I myself was convinced that I ought to do many things in opposing the name of Jesus of Nazareth. And I did so in Jerusalem; I not only shut up many of the saints in prison, by authority from the chief priests, but when they were put to death I cast my vote against them. And I punished them often in all the synagogues and tried to make them blaspheme; and in raging fury against them, I persecuted them even to foreign cities.

"Thus I journeyed to Damascus with the authority and commission of the chief priests. At midday, O king, I saw on the way a light from heaven, brighter than the sun, shining round me and those who journeyed with me. And when we had all fallen to the ground, I heard a voice saying to me in the Hebrew language, 'Saul, Saul, why do you persecute me? It hurts you to kick against the goads.' And I said, 'Who are you, Lord?' And the

Lord said, 'I am Jesus whom you are persecuting. But rise and stand upon your feet; for I have appeared to you for this purpose, to appoint you to serve and bear witness to the things in which you have seen me and to those in which I will appear to you, delivering you from the people and from the Gentiles — to whom I send you to open their eyes, that they may turn from darkness to light and from the power of Satan to God, that they may receive forgiveness of sins and a place among those who are consecrated by faith in me.'

"Wherefore, O King Agrippa, I was not disobedient to the heavenly vision, but declared first to those at Damascus, then at Jerusalem and throughout all the country of Judea, and also to the Gentiles, that they should repent and turn to God and perform deeds worthy of their repentance. For this reason the Jews seized me in the temple and tried to kill me. To this day I have had the help that comes from God, and so I stand here testifying both to small and great, saying nothing but what the prophets and Moses said would come to pass: that the Christ must suffer, and that, by being the first to rise from the dead, he would proclaim light both to the people and to the Gentiles."

And as he thus made his defense, Festus said with a loud voice, "Paul, you are mad; your great learning is turning you mad." But Paul said, "I am not mad, most excellent Festus, but I am speaking the sober truth. For the king knows about these things, and to him I speak freely; for I am persuaded that none of these things has escaped his notice, for this was not done in a corner. King Agrippa, do you believe the prophets? I know that you believe." And Agrippa said to Paul, "In a short time you think to make me a Christian!" And Paul said, "Whether short or long, I would to God that not only you but also all who hear me this day might become such as I am — except for these chains."

Then the king rose, and the governor and Bernice and those who were sitting with them; and when they had withdrawn, they said to one another, "This man is doing nothing to deserve death or imprisonment." And Agrippa said to Festus, "This man could have been set free if he had not appealed to Caesar."

Acts 26:1-32

The Apostle was brought before King Agrippa and Bernice in a formal audience. First, Festus briefly outlined how the case of St. Paul had been brought to his notice. Then Agrippa asked the Apostle to speak, and St. Paul told essentially the same story as he had from the steps leading from the Temple to the Antonia Fortress in Jerusalem. Once again he told of his persecution of the early believers, his conversion on the Damascus Road, and his appointment as Apostle to the Gentiles. He reaffirmed his theological orthodoxy by claiming that he spoke only of "what the prophets and Moses said would come to pass." As he spoke of Jesus Christ proclaiming light both to the Jews in Judaea and to the Gentiles, Festus loudly accused the Apostle of being mad. St. Paul calmly denied this assertion and continued his presentation to Agrippa. He knew the king would have the necessary background to understand his message, and he concluded with a personal appeal, "King Agrippa, do you believe the prophets? I know that you believe." Agrippa's reply — "In a short time you think to make me a Christian!" — has been interpreted in different ways. Probably Agrippa spoke sarcastically. St. Paul, however, took these words in earnest, and replied to the king, "I would to God that not only you but also all who hear me this day might become such as I am, — except for these chains." These remarks ended the session, and the king, accompanied by Bernice and the members of his council, withdrew. Agrippa believed the charges warranted neither death nor imprisonment and, had the Apostle not appealed to Caesar, he could have been set at liberty. Festus, however, had no choice. St. Paul had appealed to Caesar, and he had to be sent to Rome.

ST. PAUL'S JOURNEY TO ROME

From Caesarea to Crete

And when it was decided that we should sail for Italy, they delivered Paul and some other prisoners to a centurion of the Augustan Cohort, named Julius. And embarking in a ship of Adramyttium, which was about to sail to the ports along the coast of Asia, we put to sea, accompanied by Aristarchus, a Macedonian from Thessalonica. The next day we put in at Sidon; and Julius treated Paul kindly, and gave him leave to go to his friends and be cared for. And putting to sea from there we sailed under the lee of Cyprus, because the winds were against us. And when we had sailed across the sea which is off Cilicia and Pamphylia, we came to Myra in Lycia. There the centurion found a ship of Alexandria sailing for Italy, and put us on board. We sailed slowly for a number of days, and arrived with difficulty off Cnidus, and as the wind did not allow us to go on, we sailed under the lee of Crete off Salmone. Coasting along it with difficulty, we came to a place called Fair Havens, near which was the city of Lasea.

As much time had been lost, and the voyage was already dangerous because the fast had already gone by, Paul advised them, saying, "Sirs, I perceive that the voyage will be with injury and much loss, not only of the cargo and the ship, but also of our lives." But the centurion paid more attention to the captain and to the owner of the ship than to what Paul said. And because the harbor was not suitable to winter in, the majority advised to put to sea from there, on the chance that somehow they could reach Phoenix, a harbor of Crete, looking northeast and southeast, and winter there.

Acts 27:1-12

63

Since the Romans, whose empire was held together by the famous Roman roads, disliked the sea, and the Greeks had always been seafarers, it is not suprising that the first suitable ship leaving Caesarea was a Greek vessel from Adramyttium at the east end of the bay immediately south of Troas, which was sailing north towards its home. St. Paul and his two companions, St. Luke and Aristarchus the Macedonian from Thessalonica, were taken aboard with the other state prisoners. Aristarchus (Acts 19:29, 20:4; Col. 4:10; Philem. 24) may have been, as was St. Paul, a prisoner in the cause of Christ. The other prisoners were probably criminals destined either for the games in the Roman theaters or for the infamous sulphur mines of Sicily. The number of prisoners has been a matter of speculation. Most codices give 276, but

Caesarea: Crusader tower and part of the harbor (Acts 27:2)

this number seems very high, and two ancient codices, the Vaticanus and the Sahidic Version, mention about 76, which seems more realistic. State prisoners were often sent to Rome from the various provinces of the empire. Josephus records that Felix "for some slight offence, bound and sent to Rome several priests of his acquaintance, honorable and good men, to answer for themselves to Caesar." All were entrusted to Julius, a centurion of the Augustan Cohort, probably an auxiliary detachment stationed either in Syria or, according to Josephus, Jerusalem. It has been suggested that the centurion Julius can be identified with Julius Priscus, who later was promoted prefect of the Praetorian Guards under the Roman emperor Vitellius (69 A.D.).

The Mediterranean was considered safe for sailing from May 26 to September 14. From November 10 to March 10 the sea was officially closed because of the winter storms. The two periods from March 11 to May 25 and from September 15 to November 9 were uncertain seasons when captains avoided the open seas.

When St. Paul's ship left Caesarea the autumn of 61 was drawing on, and in a few weeks the seas would be closed for the winter. On the day after leaving Caesarea the vessel put into Sidon, the twin city of Tyre, either to take on more cargo or passengers or to shelter from strong winds which prevail in the eastern Mediterranean at the end of the summer. On the way the ship passed Ptolemais and Tyre, where St. Paul had visited with the brethren (Acts 21:3-7). During the short passage to Sidon the Apostle had already become friendly with the centurion Julius, who allowed the Apostle to go ashore and visit his friends. Stepping ashore in Sidon, St. Paul's mind would have been filled with Biblical associations from his study "at the feet of Gamaliel" (Acts 22:3). In the story of the peopling of the earth after the Flood, Sidon is mentioned as the northern border of the territory of the Canaanites (Gen. 10:15, 19). Just before his death Jacob called his sons and spoke of Sidon as "the haven for ships" (Gen. 49:13). The city's name was celebrated both in the *Iliad* and the *Odyssey* and Herodotus considered the sailors of Sidon the most experienced sailors of all the Phoenicians. We do not know the names of the friends who cared for the Apostle, but the existence of a Christian community in the city is well attested. St. Luke informs us that people from "the seacoast of Tyre and Sidon" came to hear Jesus deliver His Sermon on the Mount and "to be healed of their diseases" (Luke 6:17). Jesus Himself had visited Sidon where He healed the demon possessed daughter of a Canaanite woman (Matt. 15:21-28; Mk. 7:24-30). St. Paul and Barnabas may have passed through this city on their way from Antioch to Jerusalem (Acts 15:3), and now the Apostle had the opportunity both to strengthen the community's faith and to be comforted by them.

Sidon, known since the 7th century as Saida, today is a small southern Lebanese port whose inhabitants include a large number of Palestinian refugees. Saida's most noteworthy building is Qalaat al-Bahr, the Crusader fortress on a small island at the entrance of the northern port. It is likely that the ship on which St. Paul sailed would have anchored in this harbor, which is still used by small coastal freighters. About 6 km. southeast of Saida is the Christian pilgrimage shrine of Sayidet al-Mantara (Our Lady of Protection), which commemorates the visit of Jesus Christ to Sidon.

After leaving Sidon the ship encountered adverse winds and, instead of sailing directly across to Myra, sailed "under the lee of Cyprus" north towards the southern coast of Asia Minor. The Western Text of the Bible adds that the voyage under the mountains of Cilicia and through the bay of Pamphylia to Myra took them fifteen days. Myra was a well-known port of refuge from the seasonal storms and was often used by the large grain ships from Alexandria. At Myra the ship with its prisoners anchored in the mouth of the little river Andriace. Pliny mentions Andriace as the harbor of Myra, and the 2nd century A.D. Roman historian Appian of

Sidon: The harbor, sketch by David Roberts, 1856 (Acts 27:3)

David. Roberts. R.a.

Alexandria described the port as closed and protected by a chain. Here the centurion found another ship, probably a government vessel supplying Rome with Egyptian grain, on which Julius requisitioned passage for himself and his prisoners.

This new ship must have been one of the larger merchantmen in the Mediterranean for, in addition to her grain cargo, she had to accommodate Julius and his prisoners, bringing the full cargo weight up to between 600 and 1,000 tons. The Alexandrian corn ships usually carried one large sail on a single mast and, as all other ancient ships, were unable to head much up into the wind. Sometimes a few other small sails were used, a topsail or a storm sail, and occasionally sails were raised on small fore and mizzen masts. This particular ship had a small foresail, which was set after the ship became disabled (Acts 27:40).

Outside Myra, the ship again met contrary winds, taking several days before reaching Cnidus, opposite the island of Cos. Cnidus possessed an excellent double harbor. According to Strabo one of the harbors was a naval station which could be closed and which could berth twenty triremes. Both harbors have now silted up. In St. Paul's time, however, the city was well supplied and was an ideal place for wintering, but the captain decided to continue the voyage. The ship sailed to the south of Crete to avoid the strong northerly winds blowing down the Aegean, eventually reaching Fair Havens or Kaloi Limenes near the city of Lasea. Considering the slow progress because of the unfavorable weather conditions, the ship might have reached Fair Havens by the end of the first week of October 61. Here the ship anchored, waiting for the weather to improve. We do not know how long this wait was, but it has been suggested that the ship stayed in Fair Havens about three weeks.

Crete: Fair havens, an illustration in T.A.B. Spratt's *Travels and Researches in Crete*, London 1865 (Acts 27:8)

Fair Havens is the name of a small village, a bay, and a group of islets about five and one half miles west of Cape Leon on the southern coast of Crete. The first modern description of this Biblical site comes from Captain T.A.B. Spratt, who commanded the paddle steamer "Spitfire"

Ostia: First-century ships in the Roman harbor as depicted on the reverse of a sestertius of the emperor Nero (54-68 A.D.)

through the waters off the southern coast of Crete. In 1851 the "Spitfire" anchored where, a little more than eighteen hundred years before, St. Paul's ship had sought shelter. New Testament in hand, Captain Spratt went ashore.

> Upon the dark slaty ridge rising immediately over the western bay forming the haven, we unexpectedly found the ruins of a Greek chapel, still dedicated to St. Paul, perhaps marking the very spot where the Apostle himself used to preach to the natives of Crete when the Gospel was first planted there by him during his ship's stay. A small part of the site of the old church, enclosed by four walls of loose stones, and therefore entirely open to the heavens, is still used by the natives as a chapel.

The small white chapel commemorating the Apostle's arrival in Crete is on the brow of the hill overlooking the bay. A few yards to the west of the chapel is the traditional cave, marked by a tall wooden cross, where the Apostle stayed. The few houses of Kaloi Limenes are scattered around the bay.

The Cretans entertain a number of traditions about the Apostle's missionary work on their island. One of these is that he rid Crete of poisonous snakes. When Robert Pashly visited the island in 1834 he was told that St. Paul freed the inhabitants from wild beasts and noxious animals. A few years later Captain Spratt encountered a lay brother from a nearby monastery who told him

> that while lighting a fire on the shore, the Apostle Paul was bitten by a serpent, but it did him no harm although very venomous. From that time all snakes in Crete were charmed by St. Paul and became harmless.

Plutarch used this information, in a slightly altered form, as a point of comparison when he wrote, "it may be possible to find a country in which, as it is recorded of Crete, there are no wild animals, but a government which has not had to bear with envy and jealous rivalry or contention has not hitherto

71

existed.". Whether this Cretan tradition is a transfer of a similar story told in Melita (present-day Malta) or whether it developed in fulfillment of the promise by Jesus Christ, "Behold, I have given you authority to tread upon serpents and scorpions . . . and nothing shall hurt you" (Luke 10:19) is, of course, difficult to know.

During his stay in Fair Havens St. Paul met with the owner and the captain of the ship, and advised them of the danger of continuing the journey. He was speaking from personal experience. Three times he had been shipwrecked, and at least once he had spent twenty-four hours in the open sea, (II Cor. 11:25). The fast, the Day of Atonement or Yom Kippur at the end of September or the beginning of October (the 10th of Tisri [Lev. 16:29; 23:27]) was already past. Now seafaring was dangerous because of the autumn storms.

Crete: The Bay of Loutro (Phoenix) (Acts 27:12)

The captain of the ship and the owner, however, wished to seek a better harbor, and the centurion accepted their advice. Phoenix, now known as Loutro, several miles to the west, was a far better port for waiting out the winter. The people of Loutro maintain that the Apostle actually landed on their shores, and several travelers have pointed out the little chapel of St. Paul and the spring named after him between Loutro and Aghia Roumeli. The chapel, so the Cretans maintain, commemorates the site where the Apostle baptized his first Cretan convert. A service is held in this chapel annually on the feast of SS. Peter and Paul (June 29).

From Crete to Melite

And when the south wind blew gently, supposing that they had obtained their purpose, they weighed anchor and sailed along Crete, close inshore. But soon a tempestuous wind, called the northeaster, struck down from the land; and when the ship was caught and could not face the wind, we gave way to it and were driven. And running under the lee of a small island called Cauda, we managed with difficulty to secure the boat; after hoisting it up, they took measures to undergird the ship; then, fearing that they should run on the Syrtis, they lowered the gear, and so were driven. As we were violently storm-tossed, they began next day to throw the cargo overboard; and the third day they cast out with their own hands the tackle of the ship. And when neither sun nor stars appeared for many a day, and no small tempest lay on us, all hope of our being saved was at last abandoned.

As they had been long without food, Paul then came forward among them and said, "Men, you should have listened to me, and should not have set sail from Crete and incurred this injury and loss. I now bid you take

73

heart; for there will be no loss of life among you, but only of the ship. For this very night there stood by me an angel of the God to whom I belong and whom I worship, and he said, 'Do not be afraid, Paul; you must stand before Caesar; and lo, God has granted you all those who sail with you.' So take heart, men, for I have faith in God that it will be exactly as I have been told. But we shall have to run on some island."

Acts 27:13-24

When a light wind blowing from the south indicated a change of weather, the sailors weighed anchor in Fair Havens and sailed round Cape Matala, keeping close to shore. Everyone hoped that the southerly wind which would take them to Phoenix would hold, but instead a strong wind arose and drove the ship before it.

Under these circumstances the ship, still towing her landing boat astern, passed near Cauda (Clauda according to some texts; now called Gavdos), a small island approximately 28 miles southeast of Fair Havens. With the wind partially blocked by this island, the crew was able to hoist the dinghy aboard. The next task was to undergird the ship. Ancient ships, as several ancient writers have recorded, tended to break up in heavy seas. Virgil referred to the ships in the fleet of Aeneas as lost, some on rocks, others in quicksands, but all with hull planks loosened, and Josephus recorded that the ship from which he and his companions escaped by swimming foundered in Adria. Even the sailors on Jonah's ship on the way from Joppa to Tarshish, caught in "a great wind upon the sea . . . so that the ship threatened to break up . . . threw the wares that were in the ship into the sea to lighten it for them" (Jonah 1:4-5). To prevent such disasters, the larger ships carried lines for passing under the keel to prevent the timbers from separating as part of their emergency equipment.

The greatest danger, however, was that the ship would "run on the Syrtis," the extensive North African sand bars between Tripolitania and Cyrenaica. To keep from being

74

blown so far south the sailors lowered the sail and held the ship as best they could on a western course. The storm continued unabated and on the following day they began to lighten the ship, throwing grain overboard. This probably meant that the precaution of undergirding the ship was only partially successful and that the ship was leaking badly. On the third day the sailors and passengers "cast out with their own hands the tackle of the ship."

The overcast sky prevented the navigators from determining the ship's position and direction. It was impossible for them to know how near they were to dangerous islands or the coast. Gradually the passengers gave up all hope for survival, believing that nothing could prevent the ship from sinking. All aboard "had been long without food," either because it was impossible to prepare meals or because everybody was too seasick to eat.

In this hour of despair, St. Paul rose to comfort the passengers and crew. The Apostle, confident of his mission in Rome, reminded them of the accuracy of his advice not to sail from Crete. He then shared with them his vision of the angel of God and predicted that no life would be lost though the ship would be wrecked. St. Luke did not record the response of the captain or the sailors to these words of encouragement, but we must assume that everyone aboard must have been comforted by the words of the Jewish prisoner.

The Shipwreck

When the fourteenth night had come, as we were drifting across the sea of Adria, about midnight the sailors suspected that they were nearing land. So they sounded and found twenty fathoms; a little farther on they sounded again and found fifteen fathoms. And fearing that we might run on the rocks, they let out four anchors from the stern and prayed for day to come. And

75

as the sailors were seeking to escape from the ship, and had lowered the boat into the sea, under pretense of laying out anchors from the bow, Paul said to the centurion and the soldiers, "Unless these men stay in the ship, you cannot be saved." Then the soldiers cut away the ropes of the boat, and let it go.

As the day was about to dawn, Paul urged them all to take some food, saying, "Today is the fourteenth day that you have continued in suspense and without food, having taken nothing. Therefore I urge you to take some food; it will give you strength, since not a hair is to perish from the head of any of you." And when he had said this, he took bread, and giving thanks to God in the presence of all he broke it and began to eat. Then they all were encouraged and ate some food themselves. (We were in all two hundred and seventy-six persons in the ship.) And when they had eaten enough, they lightened the ship, throwing out the wheat into the sea.

Now when it was day, they did not recognize the land, but they noticed a bay with a beach, on which they planned if possible to bring the ship ashore. So they cast off the anchors and left them in the sea, at the same time loosening the ropes that tied the rudders; then hoisting the foresail to the wind they made for the beach. But striking a shoal they ran the vessel aground; the bow stuck and remained immovable, and the stern was broken up by the surf. The soldiers' plan was to kill the prisoners, lest any should swim away and escape; but the centurion, wishing to save Paul, kept them from carrying out their purpose. He ordered those who could swim to throw themselves overboard first and make for the land, and the rest on planks or on pieces of the ship. And so it was that all escaped to land.

Acts 27:27-44

The storm continued and the anxiety aboard increased until in the middle of the fourteenth night after leaving Crete the sailors suspected "that they were nearing land." Soundings were taken and the water was found to be 20 fathoms, about 120 feet deep. A little farther on they sounded again and found 15 fathoms. They knew that land was near, but to be thrown on rocks would mean not only the loss of the ship but also death for the crew and the passengers. Four anchors were dropped from the stern to hold the ship while still in deep water; four anchors were dropped because anchor chains were not used in St. Paul's time and anchors tied only to relatively buoyant ropes do not hold well. For the time being the ship seemed safe.

Under the pretense of laying out anchors from the bow, some sailors attempted to save their lives by leaving the ship and the passengers. They lowered the dinghy, but St. Paul told the centurion and the soldiers of their action. At once the soldiers cut the ropes of the dinghy and let it go. The prudent advice of the Apostle and the immediate action of the soldiers saved the lives of all who were aboard. The Apostle had taken command of the situation and as dawn approached he spoke to everybody on board again, reassuring them with the proverbial remark of the Lord Jesus that "not a hair is to perish from the head of any of you" (Luke 21:18). Then he urged them to eat and, setting the example, he took bread and gave thanks to God before all. St. Luke's language is reminiscent of the eucharistic formula (I Cor. 11:23,24), but there is no reason to believe that St. Paul celebrated the Last Supper on this occasion. It was an ordinary meal preceded by the customary thanksgiving.

After they had eaten they threw overboard the remains of the wheat, which probably had been spoiled by the salt water. At daybreak they did not recognize the land, but they did see a small bay with a sandy or pebbly shore, where they hoped to beach the ship. They cut the anchor lines and freed the rudders, then they hoisted the foresail, heading for the shore. Soon, however, they struck a shoal where they stuck fast and, battered by the gale, the ship began to break apart.

The soldiers, who were responsible with their lives for the state prisoners, were afraid that some would swim ashore and escape, and to prevent this they planned to kill them. It was the influence of St. Paul, if only indirectly, that saved their lives. Julius, wishing to save the Apostle's life, ordered those prisoners who could swim to jump overboard, while the rest were to make use of the broken pieces of the wreck. Thus they all got safely ashore.

St. Paul on Melite

After we had escaped, we then learned that the island was called Malta. And the natives showed us unusual kindness, for they kindled a fire and welcomed us all, because it had begun to rain and was cold. Paul had gathered a bundle of sticks and put them on the fire, when a viper came out because of the heat and fastened on his hand. When the natives saw the creature hanging from his hand, they said to one another, "No doubt this man is a murderer. Though he has escaped from the sea, justice has not allowed him to live." He, however, shook off the creature into the fire and suffered no harm. They waited, expecting him to swell up or suddenly fall down dead; but when they had waited a long time and saw no misfortune come to him, they changed their minds and said that he was a god.

Now in the neighborhood of that place were lands belonging to the chief man of the island, named Publius, who received us and entertained us hospitably for three days. It happened that the father of Publius lay sick with fever and dysentery; and Paul visited him and prayed, and putting his hands on him healed him. And when this had taken place, the rest of the people on the island who had diseases also came and were cured. They presented many gifts to us; and when we sailed, they put on board whatever we needed.

Acts 28:1-10

The translators of the Revised Standard Version of the Bible have translated Μελίτη, the Greek name of the island, as Malta. Claims and rival claims concerning the location of the shipwreck have been upheld for centuries since there are two islands which were known in Greek as Melite, Melita Illyrica (Mljet) and Melita Africana (Malta). The ambiguity regarding the site of the Apostle's shipwreck lies in the original Greek text, which has left translators disagreeing whether the storm blew down across the land from the northeast, or against the land from the southeast. Obviously the direction of the wind affects the location of St. Paul's shipwreck, but this is not the place to repeat the scholarly arguments favoring the one or the other island. Both locations are based upon Christian traditions, so I shall include a description of both sites, first of Mljet and then of Malta.

ABOUT MLJET

Mljet is the southernmost of the large Dalmatian islands separated from the Peljesak peninsula by the Mljet Channel. One of the earliest references to the island was made by Pliny the Elder (23-79 A.D.), who wrote, "twenty-five miles from Issa (Vis) is the island Corcyra (Korcula), and between it and Illyricum is Meleda, from which according to Callimachus Maltese terriers get their name." In 536 A.D. the island became part of the East Roman Empire; later it fell to the Slavs and then to the rulers of Zahumlje, who in 1151 presented Mljet to the Benedictine monks from Pulsano Abbey on Monte Gargano in Apulia. In 1333 the island was attached to the Republic of Ragusa, now Dubrovnik, which ruled through a count resident in the island's capital, Babino Polje. In the 14th and 15th centuries numerous Gothic churches were built in the parish of Babino Polje. The Benedictine monastery, vacant for many years, became a tourist hotel in 1959.

In contrast to the well-known tradition of St. Paul's shipwreck on Malta, only relatively few people have written that the Apostle was shipwrecked on Mljet. The earliest known writer to connect St. Paul with Melita Illyrica was the Byzantine Emperor Constantine VII Porphyrogenitus (913-959). His *De Administrando Imperio,* written for his son, mentions the pagan Arentani, who possessed the "island of Meleda or Malozeatae where a viper fixed itself on the finger of St. Paul who burnt it in the fire." This quotation presupposes a 10th century tradition current in Constantinople that the Apostle's shipwreck occurred on Mljet rather than on Malta.

We have no further literary evidence of the Dalmatian tradition until the beginning of the 18th century. In 1730 Father Ignazio Georgi, abbot of the 13th century Benedictine abbey in Veliko Jezero on Melita Illyrica, proposed that Biblical Melite is Melita Illyrica on the Dalmatian coast. His scholarly treatise initiated a lengthy controversy. Several refutations followed within a few years of Father Ignazio's publication, the best known being written by Giovanni Antonio Ciantar, Bonaventura Attardi, Uberto do San Gaspare, and Onorato Bres. Soon the polemics moved from

The Island of Mljet, Yugoslavia

Italy to England, where the 18th and 19th century scholars Jacob Bryant and William Falconer, the poet Samuel Taylor Coleridge, and the scholarly English church historian and hymnologist John Mason Neale expressed themselves in favor of Melita Illyrica as the site of St. Paul's shipwreck.

By the latter part of the 18th century local traditions attested to St. Paul's shipwreck on the Dalmatian coast. Thomas Watkins, traveling throughout the Dalmatian coast in 1788 reported, "I lately visited in the Isle of Croma (Locrum) a monastery founded as I am told by Richard Coeur de Lion... and yesterday a party was made for me to the Isle of Melita, upon which St. Paul was shipwrecked. An honest monk conducted me to the spot where he landed, still known by the two seas that meet there." Thirty-three years later John Madox traveled along the Dalmatian coast and wrote "... there is also an island in the Adriatic Sea named Melita or Melida, the natives claim the honour of St. Paul's first visit. They insist that the wreck took place on their shore. Scripture informs us certainly that this saint was tossed about for many days and nights in the Sea of Adria."

Several local traditions pertaining to the location of the shipwreck are maintained by the Croatian Christians on the island. Vid Vuletic Vukasovic mentioned that the people of Prozura west of Sobra hold that St. Paul's shipwreck occurred in Porto Chiave, and Bishop V. Palunko of Rodope recorded the ruins of an ancient church believed to commemorate St. Paul's shipwreck about one mile from Porto Cima Meleda, near Korita. Father Nico Ucovic of Babino Polje has placed the site of the shipwreck in the Saplunara Cove, while others have identified "St. Paul's Rock" with the site of the shipwreck below the village of Maranovici, near the island of Kosmac. In the Church of St. Paul (1935) in Babino Polje a tall statue of St. Paul holding a cross in his left hand and standing on the bow of a ship towers above the northern altar.

Three arguments are commonly cited to support the location of the Apostle's shipwreck in Melita Illyrica. The first centers around the ancient use of the term "Sea of Adria" (Acts 27:27). The Roman historian Titus Livy (59 B.C.-17

A.D.) mentioned the various seas surrounding Italy, "one of them the Tuscan, the general designation of the race, and the other Hadriatic, from Hadria, an Etruscan colony, and the Greeks know the same seas as Tyrrhenian and Adriatic." Writing about anticipated catastrophes, Lucius A. Seneca (4 B.C. -65 A.D.) prophesied: "Whenever the end comes for human affairs, when parts of the world must pass away and be abolished utterly... there will be no more Adriatic, no strait of the Sicilian Sea, no Charybdis, no Scylla." The geographer Strabo, writing in about 19 A.D., clearly defines the limits of the Adria, "whereas Adrias is the name of the inside part of the sea as far as the recess, at the present time, however, Adrias is also the name of the sea as a whole... the shape and size of the Adriatic are like that part of Italy which is marked off by the Alpine Mountains and by both seas as far as Japygia and that isthmus which is betweeen the gulfs of Tarentum and Poseidonia." A more restricted definition is given by Pliny the Elder, appointed prefect of the Roman fleet by the emperor Vespasian, who described the gulf between Italy

Mljet: Saplunara Cove

Babino Polje, Mljet: Drawing of the statue of St. Paul in the
Church of St. Paul (sculptor, Lojzika Ulman, 1968)

and Illyricum as containing "two seas, in the first part the Ionian, the more inland the Adriatic." Later writers, such as Paulus Orosius, Aethicus of Istria, and Procopius of Caesarea in the 5th and .6th centuries, considered the Adriatic Sea much more extensive, including all of the Mediterranean between Africa on the south, Sicily and Italy on the west, and Greece and Epirus on the east, so as to have Carthage (Tunis) and Ragusa (Dubrovnik) situated on the same sea. In the 1st century, however, the term "Sea of Adria" referred to roughly the same sea meant by the name today: those waters between latitudes 40° and 45° 45′ north, a length of nearly 500 miles, separating Italy from the Balkan peninsula.

The second argument advanced for locating St. Paul's shipwreck on Mljet has to do with the strong winds which drove ships into the Adriatic, of which we have many accounts. The 1st century B.C. Greek historian Diodorus Siculus referred to Acrotatus (314 B.C.), who was driven into the Adriatic, and to Xanthippus the Spartan (255 B.C.), who was drowned in the swirling waters of the Adriatic. The 1st century A.D. Latin poet M. Anaeus Lucan described the "separate seas which were caught up by the storms and carried away by the winds, the Tyrrhene Sea migrated to the Aegean, and the Adriatic moved and roared in the Ionian basic," and Flavius Josephus, who made the same journey — perhaps in the same year as the Apostle Paul — tells us in his biography: "I reached Rome after being in great jeopardy at sea. For our ship foundered in the midst of the sea of Adria, and our company of 600 souls had to swim all that night". And finally, we have the famous episode of the ship in which Richard Coeur de Lion (1192) sailed on his return from Palestine. Driven from the Mediterranean into the Adriatic by storm, his ship is said to have been wrecked off Ragusa on the island of Lacroma or Locrum where, in fulfillment of a vow, Richard dedicated a church to the Holy Virgin. According to the Dalmatian tradition, Richard was shipwrecked not far from the scene of St. Paul's shipwreck.

The third argument for locating the site of St. Paul's shipwreck on Mljet has to do with poisonous snakes. St. Luke informs us that upon his arrival on the island, St. Paul handled a viper which fastened on his hand. Without suffering any harm he shook the creature into the fire, a deed which impressed the islanders to the point that they said, "he was a god." A snake could well have bitten the Apostle's hand on Mljet, for snakes of all kinds used to abound on the island. As Fodor's Yugoslavia Guide Book states: "Mljet has one peculiar fame in that it is the only place in Europe where you will find the mongoose roaming about in liberty. The explanation for this is that long ago these little animals were imported from the East to exterminate the snakes with which the island was infested."

ABOUT MALTA

Except for the account in the Acts of the Apostles the beginnings of Christianity on Malta or Melita Africana are unrecorded. The 4th century Church Father John Chrysostom asserted in his 54th Homily that St. Paul's ministry on the island resulted in the conversion of the inhabitants, and by the 5th century the subdeacon Arator was convinced that the Apostle had consecrated Publius bishop of the island, entrusting him with the spiritual leadership of the islanders. Has Christian tradition rewarded Publius, the chief man of the island, with consecration to the episcopacy because of his reception, entertainment and hospitality for three days? The first undisputed Maltese bishop is Julianus, mentioned in the council lists of the Three Chapters Council in Constantinople in 553.

In the 1st century Malta was a dependency of the province of Sicily. Its population was largely of Phoenician origin, speaking a language unfamiliar to the Apostle Paul and St. Luke, which explains the use of the term "barbarian" in the King James Version of the Bible: "If I know not the

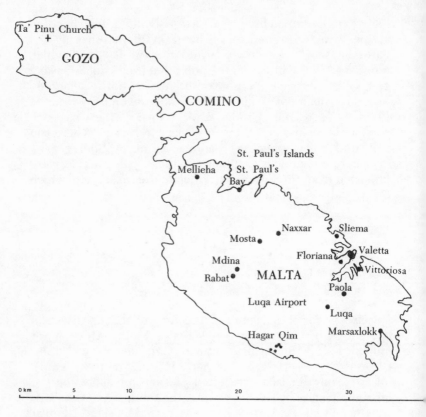

The Island of Malta

meaning of the voice, I shall be unto him that speaketh a barbarian, and he that speaketh shall be a barbarian unto me" (I Cor 14:11). These islanders, whose language they could not understand, showed them considerable kindness, for they lit a fire and welcomed the shipwrecked people to the warmth, drenched and shivering as they were in the rain and the cold.

Maltese tradition relates that as the Apostle stepped upon the island he struck a rock and caused a spring to flow from it, following the example of Moses at Mount Horeb who "lifted up his hand and struck the rock with his rod twice; and water came forth abundantly, and the congregation drank…"

(Numbers 20:11). On the mainland facing St. Paul's Island is Ghajn Rasul or the Apostle's Fountain, a small spring coming out of a rock. The Latin inscription on the marble slab above the small stream records the tradition:

> Under this hollow cliff near the seaside there is a small spring of dancing water. O traveler, venerate this water with hallowed devotion, because these waters were given to thee by the shipwrecked Paul.

News of the shipwreck rapidly spread throughout the island, and the first thing the natives did was to kindle a fire to warm the shivering strangers. Everyone joined in the search for fuel, which was scarce on the rocky terrain. As the Apostle threw his sticks into the fire, a viper slid out and bit his hand. The superstitious natives said to one another, "No doubt this man is a murderer. Though he has escaped from the sea, justice has not allowed him to live." But St. Paul threw the snake into the fire and suffered no harm. When the natives

Malta: The Place of the Two Seas, one of the traditional sites of St. Paul's shipwreck (Acts 27:41)

Malta: Ghajn Rasul, the Apostle's Fountain

saw that nothing happened to him, their feelings changed. They attributed divinity to the Apostle, but St. Paul repudiated their adoration as he had done in Lystra (Acts 14:15). He would have made use of this miracle by assigning it to the power of Jesus, especially since this event fulfilled the promise given by Jesus Christ: "I have given you authority to tread upon serpents and scorpions . . . and nothing shall hurt you" (Luke 10:19).

There is no evidence that there were poisonous snakes on Malta, and it has been suggested that this reptile was the non-poisonous Coronella Austriaka. The 16th century traveler Burchard Niderstedt reported that "the Maltese believed that St. Paul had delivered the island for ever from all such venomous serpents, in so much that children there play with scorpions ever since that time, and pilgrims daily carry with them pieces of stones out of the place where St. Paul abode, by which they affirm that they heal those which in other countries adjoining are bitten of scorpions, the medicine, therefore, being called St. Paul's grace." Monsieur de Thevenot, visiting Malta in 1655, mentioned that "no venomous creature can live there, which is a miracle the inhabitants ascribe to St. Paul, to whom they are much devoted, and believe that it is on effect of the benediction which that Saint gave after his shipwreck. They give the earth of the grott' where he was for a remedy against the stinging of serpents and other poisons, nay, against all putrid and malignant fevers also. Several barks are yearly loaded with it, to be transported into other places of Christendom."

The traditional site of St. Paul's handling of the viper is marked by the Littoral Church of St. Paul's Bay, erected by the Desguanez and Bordini families. The ancient church commemorating this miracle was destroyed by the Arabs in the 7th century. The church was rebuilt by Count Roger the Norman in 1090. In 1610 Grand Master A. Wignacourt restored the sanctuary which had fallen into decay. Partly destroyed during the Second World War, the church was reconstructed in 1956.

For three days the Apostle and St. Luke were guests of

Malta: The Littoral Church, St. Paul's Bay (Acts 28:2-6)

Publius, the chief man of the island, whose title was πρῶτος. Ancient inscriptions found on Malta confirm that this official title was common on the island, but it is not known whether Publius was a native official or a Roman representative stationed on Malta, which at that time was attached to the Roman colony of Sicily.

An extensive tract of land on the outskirts of St. Paul's Bay is known as Bu-marred or Bu-warrat, where Publius is believed to have had his property. The small rural Church of St. Paul Milqi (Welcomed) commemorates the welcome the Apostle received on the island. Archaeological excavations in 1963 on this site have brought to light some remains of the Roman period. Whereas some people identify this site with the healing of Publius's father, others maintain that the healing took place at the palace in Mdina.

Wrdija Hill (363 ft. above sea level), overlooking the neighboring lowlands and the bay, is surmounted by a small church of St. John, known as San Gwann tal-Hereb. Tradition maintains that the summit of this hill was occupied by the

Malta: The Church of St. Paul Milqi (Acts 28:7)

country estate of Publius. It is also believed that this site commemorates the baptism of Julius the Centurion of the Augustan cohort who, from the beginning of the journey, had been well disposed toward St. Paul.

On the outskirts of Naxxar is the Church of St. Paul tat-Targa, from which there is a striking view of the northern seaside. Here local tradition holds that St. Paul preached the Gospel so eloquently that the people of Gozo Island about 20 miles away heard his voice. Since the Apostle used to preach in Greek, and the inhabitants of Malta conversed in a Phoenician dialect, the Maltese believe that St. Paul made himself understood by using the apostolic "gift of tongues."

Once the apostolic party had settled in Malta they set out doing what they could do for the islanders. St. Paul's charismatic gift of healing and St. Luke's medical skills soon found scope. The father of Publius lay sick with attacks of intermittent fever and dysentery. The Apostle prayed and laid his hands on him and the patient recovered. Others who heard of this miracle soon flocked to the healers and were cured. As they were ready to depart, the islanders, grateful for these unexpected blessings, loaded the Apostle and his companions with supplies, thereby replacing at least in part what had been lost in the wreck.

In the old capital of Mdina and its lovely suburb of Rabat there are several churches and shrines which the Maltese identify with St. Paul's ministry on the island. In Mdina, the 17th century Cathedral of the Conversion of St. Paul is believed to have been built on the site of the former mansion or palace of Publius. This would have been the site, therefore, where the Apostle healed Publius's father of fever and dysentery. Maltese tradition also holds that the cathedral commemorates the consecration of St. Publius to the bishopric of Malta by St. Paul. As Father Loreto Zammit states:

Mdina, Malta: The Cathedral of the Conversion of St. Paul (Acts 28:8)

If we consider the high rank and dignity of Publius, we must believe with a certain amount of certainty that St. Paul ordained Publius bishop in the latter's palace converted afterwards into a church by St. Publius himself.

A large subterranean cave beneath the Church of St. Publius in Rabat is the traditional site of St. Paul's three month stay on the island. An early tradition maintains that St. Paul was kept in custody in this grotto, although he was permitted to preach the Gospel. The English translation of the Latin inscription in the grotto reads:

> The dark crypt which you behold benignly afforded shelter to Paul the Father and Apostle of the Gentiles, who happily was cast on this island by a shipwreck. Hence this crypt enriched by the splendid virtues of so great a man and rendered wonderful throughout the world, lest the memory of the beneficent father should diminish, it does not decrease even though stones are daily cut from it.

After the departure of the Apostle, so the islanders believe, this grotto was converted into an oratory. The white marble statue of St. Paul on the altar is the work of the Maltese artist Melchiorre Gafa. According to Father Loreto Zammit, "Nineteen centuries of history have left their mark in this venerated grotto which forms the brightest gem set in the diadem of our Pauline monuments."

Above the grotto is the early 17th century Church of St. Publius, enlarged in 1692 by Grand Master Lascaris. In this church reposes a relic of the Apostle Paul in an arm of gold, the gift of Ferdinand, Duke of Mantova, in 1620. Adjoining the Church of St. Publius is the 17th century Parish Church of St. Paul in Rabat, which commemorates the Apostle's ministry on the island. Tradition claims that the church was built on the site where the Apostle healed the infirm and preached Christ to an ever growing gathering of believers.

In Valetta, the new capital of the island, St. Paul Shipwreck Collegiate Church, though not commemorating any particular site associated with the Apostle's stay on the island, houses two relics, an arm bone of St. Paul in a silver monstrance in the form of a life size arm, and a part of the column on which the Apostle is said to have been beheaded, a gift of Pope Pius VII. Great celebrations are held annually on the 9th and 10th of February throughout Valetta in honor of St. Paul, the patron of the island.

From Melite to Rome

After three months we set sail in a ship which had wintered in the island, a ship of Alexandria, with the Twin Brothers as figurehead. Putting in at Syracuse, we stayed there for three days. And from there we made a circuit and arrived at Rhegium; and after one day a south wind sprang up, and on the second day we came to Puteoli. There we found brethren, and were invited to stay with them for seven days. And so we came to Rome. And the brethren there, when they heard of us, came as far as the Forum of Appius and Three Taverns to meet us. On seeing them Paul thanked God and took courage. And when we came into Rome, Paul was allowed to stay by himself, with the soldier that guarded him.

Acts 28:11-16

If we assume that the shipwreck occurred in the middle or toward the end of November, the departure from Melite would have taken place in February or March of the following year, 62 A.D. Pliny states that spring opens the seas to voyages when the sun is at the 25th degree of Aquarius, this date being February 8. On the other hand, according to V.R. Vegetius, sea voyages were not permitted until March 11. In all probability Julius would not have risked another stormy crossing, and it is reasonable to suggest that he sailed with his prisoners after March 11.

They were fortunate in finding another ship for Italy, probably a grain ship which had wintered on the island. The ship was named the Twin Brothers or Dioscuri, Castor and Pollux, the two children of Zeus by Leda, brothers of Helen of Troy. The two youths, whose emblem was a high cap with a star above it, were very popular among the Romans, as they were believed to have saved the state at a time of national danger. As protectors of sailors their emblem was sculptured or painted on the prow of ships named after them.

The distance from Malta to Syracuse on the island of Sicily is about eighty miles, and could have been covered in one day. Probably because of adverse winds, the Twin Brothers remained in Syracuse for three days. It is possible that some of the Galilean state prisoners aboard were transferred in Syracuse to the local Roman authorities who employed them in the sulphur mines in Gatanissetta, Girgenti, Palermo, and Catania. We are not told whether St. Paul was permitted to go ashore, though from the courtesy shown him by Julius it is probable that he did so. If he visited Syracuse, he would doubtless have found Jews and Jewish proselytes in abundance to whom he would have proclaimed the Gospel of Jesus Christ. According to St. John Chrysostom, St. Paul preached the Gospel in Sicily. The first bishop of Syracuse is believed to have been one of St. Peter's disciples, St. Marcianus, whose martyrdom is commemorated by the Orthodox Church on October 30. Syracusan tradition has identified the crypt of St. Marcianus beneath the Basilica of St. John with the site of St. Paul's preaching and his celebration of the Eucharist in the Sicilian capital. A 12th century liturgical calendar discovered by Michelangelo Mancaruso in the 17th century in the Basilica of St. John records, under the date of March 11,

> In memory of the arrival of the Apostle St. Paul who came from Malta to Syracuse with the greatest rejoicing

of the Sicilians, and enlightened the church by his preaching and his miracles.

The 4th century Bishop Germanus of Syracuse built near the Temple of Apollo in Ortygia a church of St. Paul which, after an earthquake in 1700, was rebuilt by Father Leone.

The patron saint of the Syracusans, however, is St. Lucia, who suffered martyrdom in the city during the Diocletian persecutions and whose festival is celebrated on December 13. Her relics repose in the subterranean vault beneath the Shrine of St. Lucia.

If the Apostle was permitted to stroll through the streets of Syracuse his eyes would have fallen upon the large theater and the nearby amphitheater, probably erected by Augustus, inferior in size only to the Colosseum and the amphitheaters of Capua and Verona. He would have passed by the temples of Apollo and Athena, which might have recalled to his mind his visit to Athens or that disastrous Athenian expedition (415-413 B.C.) which ended Athenian expansion toward central Italy and Europe.

At the end of three days the ship sailed from the beautiful landlocked harbor of Syracuse north toward the Straits of Messina. At first the weather seemed to be unfavorable, compelling the captain to take an indirect course. The King James Version of the Bible says that in order to get to Rhegium the sailors "fetched a compass." The most satisfactory explanation for the Greek word περιελθόντες, which the Revised Standard Version of the Bible translates as "made a circuit," may be that they tacked to Rhegium, where they stayed for one day.

By a curious coincidence the same Twin Brothers after whom the ship was named were the protectors of Rhegium and were represented on the coins of the city. Sailors often discharged their vows to the Twin Brothers in Rhegium. A tradition still upheld by the faithful in Reggio di Calabria holds that St. Paul preached on the shore during his one day stay. It was late at night and the oil lamp which provided light for the Apostle and his listeners ran dry, so St. Paul

97

miraculously lighted a column to prevent an interruption of his preaching. The column associated with this miracle and with the tying up of the ship in Rhegium is still shown in the Cathedral of Reggio di Calabria.

After awhile a south wind sprang up, favorable both for getting through the Straits and for the remainder of the journey. The Straits of Messina were dangerous because of their swift currents. Though not located by Homer, classical authors such as Strabo placed Scylla and Charybdis in the Straits of Messina, Scylla on the Italian and Charybdis on the Sicilian side. In two days, after an excellent run of about 182 miles, they reached Puteoli (modern Pozzuoli), Rome's port in the Bay of Naples. Before arriving, St. Paul must have seen Vesuvius to starboard, with its westward slope covered with vine. Who would have dreamt that the time was so near for the cities at the foot of that mountain to be enveloped in the ashes of the volcano? Who would have believed that here Drusilla, Felix's wife, who had so recently conversed with St. Paul in his prison in Caesarea (Acts 24:24), would perish with her child in the disaster of the volcano's eruption?

A description of the arrival of a ship like the Twin Brothers in Puteoli is given in the 77th Epistle by Seneca, where he speaks of the Campanians being so glad to see these Alexandrian ships:

> All the rabble of Puteoli stand on the docks, and can recognize the Alexandrian boats, no matter how great the crowd of the vessels, by the very trim of their sails. For they alone may keep spread their topsails, which all ships use when out at sea, because nothing sends a ship along so well as its upper canvas... Accordingly, when they have made Capreas (Capri) and the headland whence "Tall Pallas watches on the stormy peak" (the promontory of Minerva), all other vessels are bidden to be content with the mainsail, and the topsail stands out conspicuously on the Alexandrian boats.

When the Apostle stepped ashore in Puteoli it was

natural for him to seek out members of the Jewish community in the port city. Because of its trade with Alexandria and the East, Puteoli must have had a sizable Jewish colony which in turn would have included some Christians, who invited St. Paul to stay for seven days. We do not know the origin of the church of Puteoli. Probably some of the Roman Christians who had embraced the faith on the first day of Pentecost (Acts 2:10) proclaimed the Good News in Puteoli, which subsequently led to the establishment of a congregation. While St. Paul visited with the brethren, Julius would have sent word to the officials in Rome of his arrival in Puteoli and remained in the port city until receiving instructions how to proceed. It is even possible that Julius permitted St. Paul to address a note to the Christians in Rome announcing his arrival. Certainly the Roman Christians learned that the Apostle had arrived in Puteoli in time to come out, some to the Forum of Appius and some to the Three Taverns, to meet and welcome him.

Pozzuoli: The old harbor (Acts 28:13)

After the strenuous experiences of the past months, St. Paul would have enjoyed a vist with his fellow believers to the covered market or *macellum* of the port city. The ruins of this site, the so-called Serapeum with its massive marble and granite columns, are still visible near the new port. The famous Flavian amphitheater, seating about 40,000 spectators and the best preserved and most interesting of all the ruins in the city of Pozzuoli, was still under construction at the time of St. Paul's visit to the city.

Some say that Puteoli got its name from the wells *(putei)* while others ascribe the name to the foul smell *(puteo)* of the waters. The whole district as far as Baia and Cumae used to smell because of the sulphur and hot waters. Once known as Dicaearchia, Puteoli was still the chief port of Rome at the time of St. Paul's arrival in spite of its distance from the city. Claudius had built an artificial harbor near Rome at Ostia, but Puteoli's trade was not seriously affected. While a great part of the goods handled were grain supplies from Alexandria, Puteoli also profited from an extensive copper and bronze industry. Products of the area, known as Campania, such as olive oil, wines, and perfumes were exported and the trade with Tyre and Berytus (Beirut) was so important that these cities maintained trading colonies in Puteoli.

As in so many other places, the memory of St. Paul's week long visit is largely forgotten. The patron saint of Pozzuoli is St. Proculus and his cathedral stands in the upper city on the foundations of the Temple of Augustus, of which several columns are still visible. Although there is no church dedicated to the Apostle by the citizens of Pozzuoli, there are a high school (Liceo-Gimnasio e Collegio S. Paolo) and a bar named after the Apostle, both on the port road of the ancient harbor, which keep the memory of the Apostle's visit to Pozzuoli alive.

From Puteoli, Julius and his prisoners took the tomb

Pozzuoli: The Serapeum (Acts 28:13)

lined Consular Way which connected Puteoli with Capua, where they traveled on the so-called Queen of the Roads, the Via Appia. This great line of communication between Rome and southern Italy passed through Capua and from there to Brundisium (Brindisi) on the Adriatic coast. From Capua to Rome was a journey of five or six days for an active traveler, though we have no information how long it took Julius and his company to reach their destination. According to the 6th century Byzantine historian Procopius, writing some 800 years after the construction of the Via Appia, the road was "broad enough for two carriages to pass each other and was made of stones brought from some distant quarry and so fitted to each other that they seemed to be thus formed by nature rather than cemented by art." He adds that, despite the traffic of so many ages, the stones were not displaced nor had they lost their original smoothness. A few miles beyond Terracina, near the Sanctuary of Feronia, was the end of the Decennovium Canal, built by Augustus for draining the Pontine marshes, and which continued for some 20 miles parallel to the road as far as the Forum of Appius. Travelers could continue on the Via Appia or proceed by barges pulled by mules. We do not know the way taken by Julius and his prisoners, though no matter how they traveled, St. Paul would have seen the boatmen, tavern keepers, and the stingy landlords, eloquently described by Rome's famed 1st century B.C. poet Horace, whose interest in the place was in the comfort and entertainment, or lack of both, which it afforded to travelers. Conditions in the town would not have changed much from the days of Horace to those of St. Paul. While the Apostle was greeted by some of the brethren who had arrived from Rome, the "hideous clatter" of the boatmen along the canal preparing to move their human cargo downstream provided the background. As Horace pointed out, all hope of sleep fled because of croaking bullfrogs, buzzing mosquitoes,

Pozzuoli: St. Paul's Bar

and the singing of drunken boatmen and passengers. Today the Forum of Appius is in the small village of Borgo Faiti, and the only identification of this Biblical site is a sign, "Foro Appio," on the wall of a former 19th century customs building on the east side of the Via Appia. Nearby, on the same side of the road, is a commemorative stone with a Latin inscription which, however, is no longer legible.

About 19 km. further along the road to Rome, St. Paul was welcomed by a group of believers. The Apostle certainly must have won the full respect and confidence of Julius, for otherwise St. Paul could not have met so freely with the believers from Rome. His heart must have been lightened by the presence of these friends who accompanied him to their city. At the Three Taverns Julius and his prisoners would have made another stop. It is now believed that the Three Taverns were about 5 km. from the modern town of Cisterna Latina near the beginning of the Pontine Marshes. One of the few classical references to the Three Taverns was made by Cicero, who mentioned that on a journey from Antium to Rome he had written two letters to Atticus, one from the Forum of Appius and another, a little earlier, from the Three Taverns. St. Paul's welcome in Cisterna Latina would be forgotten today were it not for a movie theater named "Tre Taberne," which retains the memory of the Biblical site in the town.

Continuing on the Via Appia, the party passed along the base of the Alban Hills to the town of Aricia, where, as repeatedly reported by the Roman satirist Juvenal, they would have seen the swarms of beggars who beset travelers. Just outside Aricia St. Paul obtained his first view of Rome. How different from the modern Rome, without domes and belfries, without skyscrapers and the cloud of smog. About 14 km. from the capital was the ancient village of Bovillae. On either side of the road were the burial places of the Julian family, with which Julius the centurion was connected in some way. It has been suggested that Julius may have been manumitted by some member of the Julian house.

Rome: The Via Appia

105

Borgo Faiti: Site of the Forum of Appius (Acts 28:15)

The Via Appia from Bovillae to Rome was lined on either side with tombs, since Roman law prohibited burial inside the city. Approaching Rome, St. Paul passed the famous Claudian aqueduct, one of seven water channels which in Nero's day provided Rome with water, and about 2 km. further on they must have seen the Campus Rediculi, where some years before a pet crow of the Emperor Tiberius was ceremoniously buried. A little beyond was the Temple of Mars and then the burial vaults of the celebrated Scipio family, until finally they entered the city through the Porta Capena, the gate through the Servian Wall. Through this arch, perpetually dripping water from the Marcian aqueduct that passed over it, had passed all who had entered the city from the earliest days of the republic. This arch no longer exists. Today, however, the Porta San Paolo commemorates St. Paul's entry into the Eternal City.

Some scholars have estimated that St. Paul's journey from Melite to Rome took 21 days, which means that the Apostle's arrival in the capital may be dated to early April 62. On the other hand, the Western Text of the Bible informs us that upon arrival in Rome Julius went to the praetorian prefect, the commander of the praetorian guard, to whom he delivered the prisoners, while the Apostle was permitted to stay by himself with a soldier guarding him. From Tacitus we learn that ordinarily there were two prefects of the praetorian guard, but that from 51-62 A.D. there was only one prefect, Afranius Burrus, who died in January or February of 62. Since Acts refers to only one prefect, a tradition has arisen that the Apostle arrived even earlier, before the death of Burrus.

The Apostle must have been overwhelmed as he was led through this city of which he had dreamed so much. Just outside the Porta Capena he must have seen the great Circus Maximus and on his right the palaces of the Caesars on the Palatine Hill. In the middle of the circus stood the central barrier or *spina* around which the chariots raced. Here, perhaps as many as 200,000 Romans enjoyed watching the races.

Cisterna Latina: Cinema Tre Taberne (Acts 28:15)

St. Luke is silent about the place to which St. Paul was led once he entered the Eternal City. We assume that he, as were the other prisoners, was first taken to the praetorium near the Capitoline Hill, northwest of the Roman Forum. But some scholars suggest that the Biblical "prefect of the praetorian guard" was in fact the commander of the Augustan or Imperial cohort (Acts 27:1), a body of officers known as the *frumentarii* or *peregrini,* who were actually in charge of the corn supply, but also discharged police and other functions, and who resided on the Caelian Hill immediately to the east of the Porta Capena.

The Beginnings of the Church in Rome

The beginnings of the Christian Church in Rome are obscure. A persistent tradition, circulating at the end of the 2nd century, credits St. Peter with founding the Roman Church, although Clement of Rome in his *Epistle to the Corinthians* (5:3 ff.), written in 95 A.D., associated both St. Peter and St. Paul with the Church in Rome.

> Let us set before our eyes the good apostles: Peter, who because of unrighteous jealousy suffered not one or two but many trials, and having thus given his testimony went to the glorious place which was his due. Through jealousy and strife Paul showed the way to the prize of endurance; seven times he was in bonds, he was exiled, he was stoned, he was a herald both in the East and in the West, he gained the noble fame of his faith, he taught righteousness to all the world, and when he had reached the limits of the West he gave his testimony before the rulers, and thus passed from the world and was taken up into the Holy Place — the greatest example of endurance.

There is no documentary evidence from the early

109

apostolic period connecting St. Peter with the founding of the Christian community in Rome. St. Paul's letter to the Romans, written in 57 A.D. during his last visit to Corinth, indicates that the church in Rome was a strong and well established community, not of recent origin. St. Paul leaves the impression that the church was well established by the middle of the 1st century, for he wrote: "I have longed for many years to come to you" (Rom. 15:23). Had St. Peter been the founder of the Roman congregation, there almost certainly would have been some reference to his ministry in St. Paul's letter to the Romans. In chapter 1:5-15, however, St. Paul, claiming to be the Apostle to the Gentiles, assumes that Rome, being a Gentile church, lies within his apostolic jurisdiction. St. Luke informs us that St. Peter attended the Jerusalem Conference in 48 A.D. If, as he may well have done, St. Peter went to Rome after the Conference, he probably found a nucleus of Christians already worshiping there. Aquila and Priscilla arrived in Corinth from Rome probably in 49 or early 50 A.D., and they may well have been Christians before leaving the capital.

It is likely, therefore, that the church in Rome was founded by Christians converted in Palestine, perhaps the "visitors from Rome, both Jews and proselytes" (Acts 2:10), who were present at the first Christian Pentecost in Jerusalem. Roman visitors to Corinth, Ephesus, or Antioch also could have carried the Gospel back with them to Rome. Or, as Edgar J. Goodspeed suggests, "perhaps Paul, in his slow voyages about the Mediterranean, had sowed the seeds of it in conversation with strangers from Rome on the moonlit deck of some coasting vessel."

Probably the most accurate account of the beginnings of Christianity in Rome is given by a 4th century writer known as Ambrosiaster or Pseudo-Ambrose:

> It is established that there were Jews living in Rome in the times of the apostles, and that those Jews who had believed (in Christ) passed on to the Romans the tradition that they ought to profess Christ but keep the

110

law. One ought not condemn the Romans, but to praise their faith; because without seeing any signs or miracles and without seeing any of the apostles they nevertheless accepted faith in Christ, although according to a Jewish rite.

This account implies that no apostle had reached Rome before St. Paul's visit, and that lay Christians had spread the Gospel in Rome before the arrival of the "official" missionaries. Furthermore, Ambrosiaster correctly asserts that Roman Christianity had a Jewish nucleus which, however, gradually was supplanted by a Gentile congregation.

Whatever the origins of the Roman congregation, St. Paul looked forward to visiting the faithful in the Eternal City before going on to Spain.

> But now, since I no longer have any room for work in these regions, and since I have longed for many years to come to you, I hope to see you in passing as I go to Spain, and to be sped on my journey there by you, once I have enjoyed your company for a little. At present, however, I am going to Jerusalem with aid for the saints.

Rom. 15:23-25

ST. PAUL IN ROME

After three days he called together the local leaders
of the Jews; and when they had gathered, he said to
them, "Brethren, though I had done nothing against the
people or the customs of our fathers, yet I was delivered
prisoner from Jerusalem into the hands of the Romans.
When they had examined me, they wished to set me at
liberty, because there was no reason for the death
penalty in my case. But when the Jews objected, I was
compelled to appeal to Caesar — though I had no charge
to bring against my nation. For this reason therefore I
have asked to see you and speak with you, since it is
because of the hope of Israel that I am bound with this
chain." And they said to him, "We have received no
letters from Judea about you, and none of the brethren
coming here has reported or spoken any evil about you.
But we desire to hear from you what your views are; for
with regard to this sect we know that everywhere it is
spoken against."

When they had appointed a day for him, they came
to him at his lodging in great numbers. And he
expounded the matter to them from morning till
evening, testifying to the kingdom of God and trying to
convince them about Jesus both from the law of Moses
and from the prophets. And some were convinced by
what he said, while others disbelieved. So, as they
disagreed among themselves, they departed, after Paul
had made one statement: "The Holy Spirit was right in
saying to your fathers through Isaiah the prophet:
'Go to this people, and say,
You shall indeed hear but never understand,
and you shall indeed see but never perceive.
For this people's heart has grown dull,
and their ears are heavy of hearing,
and their eyes they have closed;

lest they should perceive with their eyes,
and hear with their ears,
and understand with their heart,
and turn for me to heal them.'
Let it be known to you then that this salvation of God has
been sent to the Gentiles; they will listen."

And he lived there two whole years at his own
expense, and welcomed all who came to him, preaching
the kingdom of God and teaching the Lord Jesus Christ
quite openly and unhindered.

Acts 28:17-31

The Apostle was permitted to stay by himself in his own
quarters under the supervision of a soldier who guarded him.
Three days after his arrival, St. Paul, following his usual
practice, contacted the local leaders of the Jewish community

Central Rome in St. Paul's time

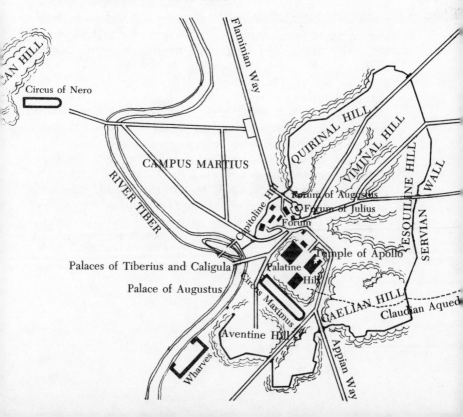

and, since he might not have been permitted to go to the local synagogue, he asked them to meet him in his rented house.

The 1st century Jewish community was centered in Trastevere, the district beyond the Tiber River. According to the satirist Juvenal it was the quarter of the poorest people and "the place of the meanest merchandise." This, then, was the home of those Jewish families who became the first Christians of Rome. The first of them had been brought to the city by Pompey as captives after his eastern campaign, and Philo records that many of them had been manumitted, so a significant proportion of these Roman Jews were free men. Their community prospered because of the trade relations with the East, and by the 1st century A.D. many Roman Jews were wealthy enough to send large sums of money annually to Jerusalem. Occasionally the Roman Jews were persecuted by the Roman authorities, as in the days of the emperor Claudius, but the community always survived. In the early years of Nero's rule, known for their leniency, the Jewish community enjoyed complete freedom, which increased their economic prosperity. The Roman Christians probably shared the immunity and protection extended to the Jews, for otherwise they would not have been able to respond so enthusiastically to the news of the Apostle's arrival in Italy.

The Jewish elders accepted St. Paul's invitation and gathered in his residence, where the Apostle explained to them why he was a prisoner, that he had committed no offence against the Jewish religion, and that he had appealed to Caesar not to accuse his own people but to save his life. In fact, his only crime had been his firm faith in God's deliverance of his people through the Messiah. "It is because of the hope of Israel that I am bound with chains." The reply of the Jewish elders was reassuring, for they had not received any word from the brethren in Judaea about the Apostle. They wished to hear more of St. Paul's religious sentiments,

Rome: The Forum

114

but added that the Christians were everywhere spoken against.

Another day was fixed for a larger meeting with the Jews, which lasted from morning till evening, again at St. Paul's private lodging. St. Paul spoke of the Kingdom of God and tried to convince his listeners that Jesus was the Christ of whom Moses and the prophets had spoken. Some believed the Apostle and some did not, and the meeting broke up after a stormy discussion. As the Jews were leaving, St. Paul admonished them for their unwillingness to accept his message by quoting almost verbatim from the Septuagint version of Isaiah 6:9-10. The Apostle must have known that his Lord had used the same words when he described those who failed to understand the meaning of His parabolic teaching (Matt. 13:14-15; Mk. 4:12; Lk. 8:10).

Paul finished his statement by stressing his intention to turn to the Gentiles. Thereafter the Apostle remained in his hired house, still in custody but free to welcome all those who came to him. He preached the Kingdom of God and taught about the Lord Jesus Christ without hindrance. The dream St. Paul had entertained in Corinth when he wrote the Roman Christians was finally realized:

> I am under obligation both to Greeks and to barbarians, both to the wise and to the foolish: so I am eager to preach the gospel to you also who are in Rome.

> Rom. 1:14-15

Here, with St. Paul triumphantly preaching in the Roman capital, St. Luke's apostolic history abruptly ends. As a result, we know very little about St. Paul's ministry in Rome during the "two whole years." An ancient tradition suggests that the Apostle and the Spanish Stoic philospher Lucius A. Seneca met in Rome. Some scholars even feel that the two men met repeatedly and were on intimate terms. A. Fleury goes so far as to write that St. Paul owed the favorable conclusion of his trial in Rome to the intervention of Seneca. He suggests, furthermore, that after being released the

Berlin, GDR: Head of Seneca, Staatliche Museen

117

Apostle traveled to Spain, for what would have been more natural than for Seneca to have wished the Gospel carried to his homeland by the same eloquent speaker with whom he had had so many discussions?

Two incidents in the Apostle's life may have led to his meeting Seneca. The first incident occurred during the reign of Claudius, perhaps in 51 A.D., when Seneca's brother Novatus, who had been adopted by their father's friend L. Junius Gallio and hence was known as Junius Gallio, served as

Rome: Bronze door of the Basilica of St. Paul-without-the-Walls with a relief depicting St. Paul on his way to Rome (sculptor, Antonio Maraini, 1931) (Acts 28:16)

proconsul of the province of Achaia. St. Luke records that the Apostle Paul was brought before Gallio by the Corinthian Jews, whom Gallio silenced (Acts 18:12-17). Gallio may have been sufficiently impressed by the Apostle at this meeting to have reported the incident to his brother, though there is nothing in the Biblical account to support such a suggestion.

The second incident is recorded only in the Western Text of the Bible, which says "the centurion handed over the prisoners to the *stratopedarch.*" The *stratopedarch* was either an officer of the praetorian guard in command of the courier troops or, more probably, the *praefectus praetorii,* the commander of the praetorian guard, who was responsible for the prisoners upon their arrival in Rome. The commander of the praetorian guard when St. Paul arrived in Rome may have been Afranius Burrus. Burrus was a good friend of Seneca's, who at that time was at the peak of his political influence. Seneca and Burrus were reluctant accessories to the assassination of the empress Agrippina in 59, and it was Seneca who composed Nero's explanation to the Roman Senate. Burrus may have spoken to Seneca about the Apostle, and Seneca may have sought St. Paul's company, for both men shared many convictions and ideas. H.V. Morton elaborates on this point when he writes: "To their cultured outlook they added, each in his own way, the concern of men conscious that a world morally bankrupt must find a new way of life. It is tempting to imagine those occasions on which Seneca may have passed from his covered litter into the 'hired house' of St. Paul."

Although St. Jerome (340-420) mentioned Seneca's correspondence with the Apostle, the earliest manuscripts of the eight apocryphal letters by Seneca to St. Paul and the six letters by the Apostle to Seneca — all indicating Seneca's conversion to the Christian faith — do not appear until the 7th century. Afterwards this tradition became widely accepted as historical fact. This chronology means that the correspondence between St. Paul and Seneca alluded to by St. Linus, St. Augustine, and St. Jerome should not be identified with the fourteen letters. All that St. Jerome states in his *De viris illustribus* 12 is:

119

L. Annaeus Seneca from Cordoba, disciple of the Stoic Sotion and uncle of the poet Lucan, led a particularly sober life. I should not include him in the list of saints, if Paul's letters to Seneca and Seneca's letters to Paul, which are read by many, did not give me just cause. Although he was Nero's tutor and very powerful in his day, he says that he would like to occupy that place among his own people that Paul occupied among the Christians. He was put to death by Nero two years before Peter and Paul received the crown of martyrdom.

In contrast to the Christian tradition, there is nothing in the extant writings of Seneca, which are from all periods of his life, indicating that Seneca ever met the Apostle or in any way was influenced by the Christian Gospel.

Several traditions have identified different locations with the site of the Apostle's hired house in Rome. A medieval tradition places the 7th or 8th century Church of St. Maria in Via Lata (entrance at 306 Via del Corso) on the site of St. Paul's Roman residence. Above the entrance to the ancient subterranean oratory is the Latin text of Acts 28:16 "And when we came into Rome, Paul was allowed to stay by himself, with the soldier that guarded him," although the tradition states that St. Paul stayed there together with St. Peter, St. Luke, and St. Martial, as depicted by a medieval marble relief in the subterranean oratory. A medieval legend informs us that St. Martial, the companion of St. Peter in Rome, was one of the Seventy Disciples of Jesus Christ, and was sent by St. Peter from Rome to Gaul.

On the Aventino, between the Porta San Paolo and the Circus Maximus, is the Church of Santa Prisca on the Via Santa Prisca. Another Roman tradition, based on the assumption that Aquila and Priscilla were living in Rome

Rome: Church of Santa Prisca (Acts 28:30)

during St. Paul's imprisonment, considers the subterranean oratory discovered in the late 18th century near this church as the site of St. Paul's hired house. On the other hand, G. Parisi argues that the "hired house" was near the present Ponte Garibaldi, marked by the Church of San Paolo alla Regola.

St. Paul's presence in Rome, although not his hired house, is also remembered by another early Christian tradition. The Church of Santa Pudenziana in the Via Urbana at the foot of the Esquiline near the Church of Santa Maria Maggiore was built on the site where SS. Peter and Paul were entertained by Pudens according to the tradition developed from the reference in II Tim. 4:21. This church is believed to be the oldest in Rome, and contains the earliest mosaic portraits of the two Apostles. The crypt of the church is said to be the house where Pudens and his daughters Praxedis (Prassede) and Pudentiana offered hospitality to the early Roman Christians. Concerning it, H.V. Morton writes, "There can be no doubt that this house existed when St. Paul was in Rome. It is possible that he entered it and that the very walls which rise up round one in the dark echoed to the sound of his voice."

During his stay in Rome St. Paul probably met several Christians whom he admonished to preach the Gospel in Italy. For example, a local tradition in Arrezo, the ancient Arretium, in Tuscany, states that St. Romulus, a disciple of St. Paul, introduced the Gospel in the town. Later St. Paul consecrated St. Romulus bishop of Fiesole.

St. Luke does not inform us of the outcome of St. Paul's appeal to Caesar. Some scholars maintain that after his two year residence St. Paul was executed, as a Roman citizen, perhaps on the charge of sedition against the government rather than on the ground of preaching new gods or promulgating an illegal religion. After all, they argue, the original accusation by the Jews that "this man (is) a pestilent

Rome: Church of San Paolo alla Regola (Acts 28:30)

fellow, an agitator among all the Jews throughout the world, and a ringleader of the sect of the Nazarenes (who) even tried to profane the temple" (Acts 24:5,6) was not withdrawn. During the later years of Nero's reign such a crime certainly would have been punished severely, and could easily have resulted in St. Paul's execution.

Early Christian tradition, however, maintained that St. Paul fulfilled his intention to visit Spain and that he was rearrested, convicted, and condemned to death during the Neronian persecutions when he returned to Rome. If this were the case, the Apostle would have been released after the two year period in custody, and since the Jews had received no letters from Judaea following up the incident, the charges against him may have been dropped by default.

ST. PAUL'S JOURNEY TO SPAIN

We will probably never know whether or not St. Paul fulfilled his intention expressed in his letter to the Romans to visit Spain, "I hope to see you in passing as I go to Spain" (Rom. 15:24), and "I shall go on by way of you to Spain" (Rom. 15:28). The Early Church believed that the Apostle's appeal to Caesar was successful, that he was acquitted of the charges against him, and that he spent some years in freedom before he was again imprisoned and sentenced to death. The 4th century church historian Eusebius wrote that "after pleading his cause, he is said to have been sent again upon the ministry of preaching, and after a second visit to the city, that he finished his life with martyrdom" (Hist. Eccl. II, xxii).

Evidence of St. Paul's activity after the "two whole years" mentioned in Acts 28:30 is found in three early Christian documents. In 96 A.D. St. Clement of Rome — whom tradition has identified with St. Paul's disciple mentioned in Phil. 4:3 — wrote in a letter to the Corinthians that St. Paul

> had been seven times in bonds, had been driven into exile, had been stoned, had preached in the East and in the West, he won the noble renown which was the reward of his faith, having taught righteousness unto the whole world and having reached the farthest bounds of the West...

For a Roman author, the "farthest bounds of the West" meant Spain. Further evidence of St. Paul's journey to Spain is in the late 2nd century Acts of Peter, the first three chapters of which give details of St. Paul's departure from the harbor of Ostia for Spain. The third early Christian document mentioning St. Paul's Spanish mission is the *Muratori Canon,* compiled by an anonymous author about 170 A.D. This document, originally written in Greek and then badly translated into Latin, says of the Acts of the Apostles that

Luke puts it shortly to the most excellent Theophilus that the several things were done in his own presence, as he also plainly shows by leaving out the passion of Peter and also the departure of Paul from Town on his journey to Spain.

We will not discuss here the arguments for or against the Apostle's journey to Spain, but by the end of the 2nd century most Christians believed that the Apostle had in fact visited Spain. Exaggeration of historical fact is an ancient practice. In I Maccabees 1:3 it is said that Alexander the Great "went through to the ends of the earth," and in the *Excerpta Latina Barbari* we read that "he subjugated all races from the Caspian Gates which are in the orient, to the outer bounds of Hercules, which are in the extreme regions over against Cadiz." In the romance of Alexander by the 3rd century A.D. Pseudo-Callisthenes a detailed account is given of Alexander's journey to Ethiopia, which the king at one time had planned, but which, in fact, he never undertook. Many other such examples could be cited. It could easily be that the tradition of St. Paul's mission to Spain is such a fabrication. St. John Chrysostom, however, mentions the Apostle's journey as an undoubted historical fact, that "Paul after his residence in Rome departed to Spain," and St. Jerome believed that the Apostle reached Spain by sea.

We shall assume that St. Paul did in fact realize his plans to visit Spain. In that case he would have traveled from Rome along the Via Ostiensis to Ostia, the new port of imperial Rome begun by Claudius and dedicated by Nero in 54 A.D. as Portus Augusti. The port soon became one of the larger cosmopolitan and commercial centers in Italy, with more than 50,000 inhabitants. According to Strabo, "it was the port-town of the Roman navy, the port into which the Tiber, after flowing past Rome, empties." Every year on January 27, large crowds from Rome and its environs gathered in Ostia for the celebrations in honor of Castor and Pollux. The Jewish community maintained a synagogue on the edge of the city on the Via Severiana. Excavations of the synagogue have revealed an elaborate vestibule leading to the main building, ending in a slightly curved apse. In the southern section was the tabernacle, containing the scrolls of the Hebrew Scriptures. St. Paul may have visited and even preached in this synagogue.

Ships sailed regularly from Ostia to Cadiz and Tarraco, now known as Tarragona. According to Pliny the Elder, who served as procurator in the province of Hispania Tarraconensis under Vespasian, the journey from Ostia to Spain took four days. The third chapter of the apocryphal Acts of St. Peter vividly describes the departure of the Apostle Paul from Ostia harbor:

> A great multitude of women were kneeling and praying and beseeching Paul, and they kissed his feet and accompanied him unto the harbor. But Dionysius and Balbus of Asia, knights of Rome, and illustrious men, and a senator by name Demetrius abode by Paul on his right side and said: "Paul, I would desire to leave the city if I were not a magistrate, that I might not depart from thee." Also from Caesar's house Cleobius and Iphitus and Philostrate with Narcissus the presbyter accompanied him to the harbor: but whereas a storm of the sea came on, he (Narcissus?) sent the brethren back to Rome, that if any would, he might come down and hear Paul until he set sail; and hearing that, the brethren went up unto the city. And when they told the brethren that had remained in the city, some on beasts, and some on foot, and others by way of the Tiber came down to the harbor, and were confirmed in the faith for three days, and on the fourth until the fifth hour, praying together with Paul, and making the offering, and they put all that was needful on the ship and delivered him two young men, believers, to sail with him, and bade farewell in the Lord and returned to Rome.

Tarragona would have been the most likely city for St. Paul's mission in Spain. To commemorate the victories of

127

Julius Caesar, the city became known as Colonia Julia Victrix Triumphalis Tarraco and was made the seat of one of the four assize courts established in the province of Hispania Citerior. The emperor Augustus had spent some time in Tarragona and had made it the capital of the province, which received the name of Hispania Tarraconensis. East of the site of the present cathedral the people of Tarragona had built an altar to Augustus.

An 8th century tradition relates that St. Paul consecrated St. Prosperus first bishop of Tarragona. Because of local persecutions, St. Prosperus fled to Regium Lepidum — modern Reggio Nell' Emilia, northwest of Bologna — where he was immediately accepted as bishop of the city "because he is the successor of St. Paul in Tarragona." The 10th century Greek *Menologian* and the *Hagiography of Symeon Metaphrastes* mention that St. Paul converted the two sisters Xanthippe and Polyxene, who are commemorated in the Greek Orthodox Church on September 23. Xanthippe was the wife of Philotheus, prefect of Provo (?), whom she converted to the Christian faith. Polyxene, on the other hand, went to Achaia in Greece, where she was perfected in the faith when she received the baptism from St. Andrew the First-called.

Although one of the two patrons of Tarragona is St. Fructuosus, an early bishop of the city who, together with SS. Eulogius and Auguris, suffered martyrdom in the local amphitheater in 259 A.D., St. Paul is commemorated by the Catalanians. Behind the Metropolitan Cathedral, in the cloister of the 19th century Diocesan Seminary, is the old chapel of St. Paul, said to have been built on the site of the Apostle's preaching in Tarragona. The foundation walls belong to the Roman period, the upper part to the medieval age. On the Plaza de Palacio, next to the Metropolitan Cathedral, built over the remains of the once lofty temple of Jupiter-Ammon, stands a statue of St. Paul erected in 1963 on

Tarragona: The Forum

the occasion of the 19th centenary celebrations of St. Paul's preaching to the citizens of Tarragona.

The co-patron of Tarragona is St. Thecla, whose right arm is said to repose in her chapel in the cathedral. In the principal sanctuary of the cathedral the white marble front of the high altar shows eight magnificent 12th century reliefs of scenes depicting the romantic story of SS. Paul and Thecla in Iconium (Konya) in Asia Minor. A feast in honor of St. Thecla is celebrated annually on September 23. In Tortosa, 55 km. west southwest of Tarragona on the River Ebro, a tradition claims that St. Paul as founder of the local church consecrated St. Rufus, the son of Simon of Cyrene (Mark 15:21; Rom. 16:13) first bishop of the city. Like Tarragona, Tortosa was a Roman colony and was known as Julia Augusta Dertosa in Hispania Tarraconensis.

In addition to Catalan traditions of the visit of St. Paul to Spain there is an Andalusian cycle of legends which is maintained by the church in Ecija (Astigis) in the province of Seville. These 16th century traditions hold that the Apostle sailed from Ostia to Cadiz from which he proceeded to the Roman colony of Astigis, known as Augusta Firma. It is claimed that St. Hierotheus, a citizen of Astigis, was converted by the Apostle Paul in Athens, where he became the city's first bishop. Later, St. Hierotheus consecrated St. Dionysius the Areopagite bishop of Athens and asked St. Paul to visit his native city. After his first Roman imprisonment St. Paul came to Astigis where he preached in the forum, converting many people. He consecrated St. Crispin, patron of shoemakers, bishop of Astigis. It is no coincidence that Ecija was famous throughout Spain for its shoemakers. On January 25 the citizens gather in the Church of the Holy Cross and St. Paul to commemorate both the Apostle's ministry in Spain and his apparition in the Church of St. Barbara in 1436.

None of the local Spanish traditions can be traced to

Tarragona: The Chapel of St. Paul in the Diocesan Seminary

AL APOSTOL SAN PABLO
EN EL XIX CENTENARIO
DE SU VENIDA A ESPAÑA
Y DE SU ESTANCIA EN TARRAGONA

MCMLXIII

AÑO JUBILAR CONCEDIDO
POR S. S. JUAN XXIII
F. M.

TRESCIENTOS DIAS DE INDULGENCIA
A CUANTOS RECEN DEVOTAMENTE
UN PADRENUESTRO,
AL PASAR ANTE ESTA IMAGEN.

+ B. CARD. DE ARRIBA Y CASTRO

before the 8th century; most of them emerged during the 14th century or later. In the early nineteen-sixties several Spanish communities celebrated the 19th centenary of the arrival of the Apostle in Spain and in 1961 the Spanish postal authorities issued a one peseta commemorative stamp showing El Greco's St. Paul with the text: XIX CENTENARIO DE LA VENIDA DE SAN PABLO A ESPANA.

Spanish postage stamp commemorating the 19th centenary of St. Paul's arrival in Spain.

Tarragona: Statue of St. Paul on the Plaza de Palacio

ST. PAUL'S MARTYRDOM

The New Testament records are silent about the Apostle's last years and the manner of his death. We have concluded that St. Paul arrived in Rome in 62 A.D. and St. Luke mentions that "he lived there two whole years" (Acts 28:30), after which he may have been released. We have assumed that he went to Spain and returned to Rome to continue his mission "to all God's beloved in Rome, who are called. to be saints" (Rom. 1:7).

The earliest possible testimony of St. Paul's martyrdom is St. Clement's letter to the Corinthians, written from Rome in 96 A.D. In this account, the Bishop of Rome does not attempt a history of events, but merely cites the event to illustrate the suffering caused by jealousy and envy, assuming that the details were well known to his readers in Corinth.

> By reason of jealousy and strife Paul by his example pointed out the prize of patient endurance . . . And when he had borne his testimony before the rulers, so he departed from the world and went unto the holy place, having been found a notable pattern of patient endurance. Unto these men of holy lives was gathered a vast multitude of the elect, who through many indignities and tortures, being the victims of jealousy, set a brave example among ourselves. By reason of jealousy women being persecuted, after they had suffered cruel and unholy insults as Danaids and Dircae, safely reached the goal in the race of faith, and received a noble reward, feeble though they were in body.

There is no doubt that these events described by St. Clement of Rome refer to the Neronian persecutions, for, so far as it is known, there was no persecution of "a vast multitude of the elect" before the Domitian persecution other than the Neronian. Tacitus, writing about the Neronian persecutions, confirmed the statement by St. Clement that a vast multitude of Christians were being put to death with insult, dressed up in the skins of beasts to be killed by dogs.

Eusebius clearly speaks of a second visit of St. Paul to Rome where he finished his life in martyrdom during the 13th year of Nero's reign, 67 A.D.

> Thus Nero publicly announcing himself as the chief enemy of God, was led in his fury to slaughter the apostles. Paul is therefore said to have been beheaded at Rome, and Peter to have been crucified under him. And this account is confirmed by the fact that the names of Peter and Paul still remain in the cemeteries of that city to this day.

Details of the last days and hours of the Apostle's life are given by the 2nd century apocryphal Acts of Paul. Here three distinct episodes describe St. Paul's mission to the emperor's

Emperor Nero (54-68 A.D.) depicted on obverse of bronze Roman sestertius

household and to the emperor himself: the hiring of a house for missionary work, the calling back to life of Patroclus — an obvious parallel to the story of the calling back to life of Eutychus in Troy (Acts 20:7-12) — and St. Paul's appearance before Caesar, in fulfillment of the prophecy by Jesus Christ: "you will stand before governors and kings for my sake, to bear testimony before them" (Mark 13:9).

When Paul saw them (his friends) he was glad and hired a grange outside Rome, wherein with the brethren he taught the word of truth and he became noised abroad and many souls were added unto the Lord, so that there was a rumour throughout all Rome, and much people came unto him from the household of Caesar, believing, and there was great joy.

Patroclus, a cup bearer of Caesar, came unto the grange, and not being able because of the press to enter in to Paul, he sat in a high window and listened to him teaching the word of God. But whereas the evil devil envied the love of the brethren, Patroclus fell down from the window and died, and forthwith it was told unto Nero. Then Paul called on the congregation, "Now, brethren, let your faith appear, come all of you and let us weep unto our Lord Jesus Christ, that this lad may live." And when all had lamented, the lad received his spirit again, and they set him on a beast and sent him back alive.

When Patroclus returned to the palace he witnessed to the emperor about the miracle and the power of Jesus Christ which raised him from the dead. Thereupon Patroclus together with Barsabus Justus of the broad feet and Urion the Cappadocian and Festus the Galatian, Caesar's chief men, were slain for their faith.

Ostia: The ruins of a Roman two-story house, like the one from which Petroclus is reported to have fallen

Later, the Apostle was brought before Nero, in the emperor's palace, the Golden House which he had built with lavish splendor after the burning of Rome in 64. The palace grounds were on such a magnificent scale that the emperor Vespasian was later able to build the Colosseum on the site of an artificial lake in Nero's palace gardens. The tradition continues with St. Paul's words:

"O Caesar, not only out of thy province do we levy soldiers, but out of the whole world. For so hath it been ordained unto us, that no man should be refused who wishes to serve my king...It is not wealth nor the splendour that is now in this life that shall save thee, but if thou submit and entreat Him, thou shalt be saved, for one day He shall fight the world with fire." When Caesar heard this, he commanded all the prisoners to be burned with fire, but Paul to be beheaded after the law of the Romans. But Paul did not keep silence, and communicated with Longus the prefect and Cestus the centurion.

The privileges of Roman citizenship exempted St. Paul from the painful death of lingering torture. According to the medieval Martyrology of Baronius under March 4, St. Paul was detained in the notorious Mamertinum or Mamertine Prison, also known as the Carcer, the ancient state prison at the foot of the Capitoline Hill. The ancients described the place with horror, and the 1st century B.C. Roman historian Sallust described the Carcer in his narrative of the execution of Catiline as "exceeding dark, unsavory, and able to craze any man's senses." Both King Jugurtha of Numidia and the Gallic chieftain Vercingetorix died in this dungeon.

The upper room is a vaulted trapezoid where a part of the column to which St. Paul was tied is exhibited. In the subterranean chamber, originally accessible only by a hole, the prisoner was kept. It was here where, according to a late tradition, a spring of water gushed forth, providing the Apostle with water for baptizing the prison guards, an obvious parallel to the conversion and baptism of the jailer in Philippi

138

(Acts 16:25-34). The upper portion of the building is now occupied by the Church of San Guiseppe dei Falegnami (St. Joseph the Carpenter).

Some scholars believe that during this second Roman imprisonment St. Paul wrote the Second Letter to Timothy. He was no longer optimistic, as he had appeared to be in his other letters. On the contrary, he considered the situation hopeless and sent his farewell greetings.

> For I am already on the point of being sacrificed; the time of my departure has come. I have fought the good fight, I have finished the race, I have kept the faith. Henceforth there is laid up for me the crown of righteousness, which the Lord, the righteous judge, will award to me on that Day, and not only to me but also to all who have loved his appearing.
>
> II Tim. 4:6-8

Rome: Sign above entrance to the Mamertinum

Only one of his friends, St. Luke, stayed with him (II Tim. 4:10-11). Demas, in love with this present world, had deserted him and gone to Thessalonica, Crescens had gone to Galatia, and Titus to Dalmatia. Other friends, however, were able to visit the Apostle. Onesiphorus, one of his friends from Asia, had diligently sought him out and visited him in prison, undeterred by fear of danger or shame (II Tim. 1:16-17). Linus, afterwards bishop of the Church of Rome, called on him to receive his blessings, and so did Pudens and Claudia (II Tim. 4:21). Some people maintain that Pudens and Claudia were the couple mentioned in the two epigrams (IV, 3; XI, 54) by the 1st century A.D. Roman epigrammatist Marcus V. M. Martial. The first epigram describes the marriage of Pudens, a distinguished Roman, to Claudia, a foreign lady. The second epigram informs us that

> Claudia Rufina may be a blue-eyed Briton born, how much has she the disposition of the Latin race. The Italian matrons might believe her a Roman, those of Attica of their country. The gods bless her in that she proves fruitful to her pious husband.

These epigrams were written during Martial's residence in Rome, sometime between 66 and 100 A.D.

This imprisonment was evidently more severe than his previous one, and none of his friends stood by him in the court of justice (II Tim. 4:16). We do not know the precise charge made against St. Paul. Probably he was accused of propagating a new and illicit religion among the citizens of Rome. He may also have been charged with instigating the supposed act of incendiarism, the burning of the city, for which the Christians were blamed. Alexander the coppersmith was one of his accusers or, at least, a witness against him (II Tim. 4:14).

The first stage of the trial would have been conducted by a magistrate appointed by the emperor and controlled by a council of assessors. The trial took place before a large audience, for "the Lord stood by me and gave me strength to proclaim the word fully, that all the Gentiles might hear it" (II

Rome: Marble relief, donated in 1867 by Pope Pius IX
(1792-1878), in the Church of Tre Fontane, depicting the
decapitation of St. Paul (artist unknown)

Tim. 4:17). He may have been tried in one of the two great
Pauline basilicas, which received their name from the
well-known Roman general Lucius Aemilus Paulus, who had
built one of them and restored the other. As W. J. Conybeare
suggests, "It is not impossible that the greatest man who ever
bore the Pauline name was tried in one of them."

According to the report by the Roman presbyter Caicus (ca. 200) and recorded by Eusebius, St. Paul suffered martyrdom on the Via Ostiensis. As he passed through the Porta Ostiensis, later known as the Porta San Paolo, he must have passed the sepulchral pyramid of Gaius Cestius. Where the basilica of St. Paul's-without-the-Walls now stands, he was led off onto the Via Laurentia. He was martyred at the "third milestone from the city," known in ancient times as Aquae Salviae (Salvian Waters), and later as Tre Fontane (Three Fountains). The apocryphal Acts of Paul describe his martyrdom with these words:

> Then Paul stood with his face to the east and lifted up his hands unto heaven and prayed for a long time, and in his prayer he conversed in the Hebrew tongue with the fathers, and then he stretched forth his neck without speaking. And when the executioner struck off his head, milk spurted upon the cloaks of the soldiers. And the soldiers and all that were there marvelled and glorified God and they told Caesar what was done.

The local tradition asserts that as the head of the Apostle was severed from his body it bounced three times as it rolled down the slight incline, and on each of these three spots a fountain is said to have miraculously sprung. The Trappist Monastery of Tre Fontane, situated in a pine wood, is the oldest monastery in Rome. It encloses three churches, two of which are associated with the martyrdom of the Apostle. The foundations of the Church of Tre Fontane, built on the site of the Salvian Springs, go back to the early Christian period, for when Pope Sergius I had the church repaired in 689 it was already crumbling. The ancient building was demolished and replaced by the present church in 1599 by Cardinal Pietro Aldobrandini, at that time Commendatory Abbot of Tre

Rome: Entrance to the Church of Tre Fontane

Fontane. The three fountains, sealed up in 1950, are in line and equally spaced along the entire length of the nave. In the corner between the altar of St. Paul and the first fountain a marble column is preserved, which is said to be the actual milestone to which the Apostle was fastened when he was beheaded. Inside the little church, which has been recently redecorated, and covering the wall of the apse behind the middle fountain there is a large painting of the martyrdom of St. Paul. The second church, known as Scala Coeli, is built over a crypt which tradition has identified with the dungeon where the Apostle was imprisoned while awaiting his execution.

A noble matron named Lucina buried the Apostle on her own land, the *praedio Lucina,* near the Via Ostiensis. Today this ancient cemetery is near the Basilica of St. Paul-without-the-Walls. In the 3rd century the bodies of SS. Peter and Paul were temporarily removed to prevent an attempt by some Jewish Christians to steal the bodies and carry them to the East. For a number of years the remains of the two apostles reposed in a niche in the marble tomb, the Platonia, in the catacomb of St. Sebastian on the Via Appia. Later the body of St. Paul was returned to the Via Ostiensis.

Constantine the Great transformed the former *cella memoria* of St. Paul into a large basilica and Pope Sylvester I is said to have consecrated the Basilica of St. Paul-without-the-Walls on the same day on which the Basilica of St. Peter at the Vatican was consecrated, November 18, 324. The church was several times enlarged and rebuilt. St. Paul's-without-the-Walls and St. Peter's soon became the most famous pilgrimage shrines in Western Christendom. On the night of July 15, 1823, when Pope Pius VII, formerly a monk at St. Paul's, lay dying, a disastrous fire broke out and left very little of the basilica standing. The 13th century tabernacle, part of the beautiful facade, the triumphal arch, the trancept, and

Rome: Church of St. Paul-without-the-Walls

the cloister were saved from the flames, but the famous 13th century frescoes by Cavellini were destroyed and the mosaics gravely damaged. The tomb of St. Paul was one of the few uninjured objects in the church. One feature of the tomb revealed by the destruction and since kept visible under the high altar is a 4th century inscription carved on a marble slab:

PAVLO

APOSTOLOMART

According to Rodolfo Lanciani, who examined the tomb in 1891, "the grave of St. Paul has come down to us, most likely, as it was left by Constantine the Great, enclosed in a metal case. The Saracens of 846 damaged the outside marble casing and the marble epitaph, but did not reach the grave. As to the nature of the grave itself, its shape, its aspects, its contents, I am afraid our curiosity will never be satisfied."

Gifts for the reconstruction of the basilica poured in from all quarters of the earth and in 1854 the basilica was consecrated by Pope Pius IX. The interior of the 19th century basilica follows the general plan of the earlier church. Eighty monolithic granite columns divide the church into five aisles. The frescoes represent scenes of the Old and New Testaments and of the life of St. Paul, and a series of medallions with portraits of the popes runs along the walls of the aisles on the cornice above the arches.

The relics of the Apostle repose in the tomb, which was visible until the 9th century, when it was walled up. It was rediscovered during the restoration works carried out in the 19th century. The skulls of SS. Peter and Paul are encased in a reliquary above the papal altar in the Basilica of St. John in Laterano. The eight iron links with which St. Paul is believed to have been chained are exhibited in the sacristy of the Basilica of St. Paul-without-the-Walls.

For our deeper understanding and appreciation of the Apostle Paul, however, basilicas and relics are secondary. It is fitting to end this text with St. Paul's message to the

Christians of Rome. He had lived as an apostle, saint, witness, confessor, and martyr, and was able to say:

> For I am sure that neither death, nor life, nor angels, nor principalities, nor things present, nor things to come, nor powers, nor height, nor depth, nor anything else in all creation, will be able to separate us from the love of God in Christ Jesus our Lord.

Romans 8:38-39

Rome: The tomb of St. Paul in St. Paul-without-the-Walls

BIBLIOGRAPHY

Balmer, Hans. *Die Romfahrt des Apostel Paulus und die Seefahrtskunde im römischen Kaiserzeitalter.* Bern, 1905.

Barlow, Claude W., ed. "Epistolae Senecae ad Paulum et Pauli ad Senecam 'Quae vocantur.'" In *Papers and Monographs of the American Academy in Rome,* X, 1938.

Bertelli, C. and Paluzzi, C.G. *S. Maria in Via Latina.* Rome, 1971.

Bornkamm, Günther. *Paulus.* Stuttgart, 1969.

Boyer, David S. "Jerusalem to Rome in the Path of St. Paul." *National Geographic,* December, 1956.

Cali, Raphael Bonnici. *Our Lady of Mellieha.* Valetta, 1952.

Catania, F. *Footprints of St. Paul in Malta.* Malta, 1913.

Clermont-Ganneau, Ch. "Une stèle du Temple de Jérusalem." *Revue Archéologique,* XXIII, 1872, pp. 214-234.

Davies, Ll. *St. Paul's Voyage to Rome.* London, 1931.

Dittenberger, W. *Orientis Graeci Inscriptiones Selectae.* Leipzig, 1905.

Du Bois, Ch. *Pouzzoles Antique. Paris, 1907.*

Dubowy, Ernst. "Klemens von Rom über die Reise Pauli nach Spanien." *Biblische Studien,* XIX, 3, 1914.

Falconer, W. *Dissertation on St. Paul's Voyage from Caesarea to Puteoli, and on the Apostle's Shipwreck on the Island of Melite.* London, 1872.

Fleury, A. *St. Paul et Sénèque.* Paris, 1853.

Forbes, S. Russell. *The Footsteps of St. Paul in Rome.* London, 1882.

Georgi, Ignazio. *Divus Paulus Apostolus in mari, quod nunc venetus sinus dicitur, naufragus, et Melitae Dalmatenses insulae post naufragiam hospes, sive de genuino significatu duorum locorum in Actibus apostolicis cap. 27:27, cap. 28:1 inspectiones anticriticae.* Venice, 1730.

Goodspeed, Edgar J. *An Introduction to the New Testament.* Chicago, 1937.

Hicks, E.L. "Philip the Evangelist and the Epistle to the Hebrews." *The Interpreter,* 1908-1909, pp. 245-265.

James, Montague R. *The Apocryphal New Testament.* Oxford, 1926.

Knox, John. "The Epistle to the Romans." *The Interpreter's Bible,* IX, Nashville, 1954.

Lanciani, Rudolfo. *Pagan and Christian Rome.* New York, 1892.

Macgregor, G.H.C. "The Acts of Apostles." *The Interpreter's Bible,* Nashville, 1954.

Mackinnon, Albert G. *The Rome of St. Paul.* London, 1930.

Madox, John. *Excursion in the Holy Land, Egypt, Nubia and Syria.* London, 1834.

Mayr, Albert. "Zur Geschichte der älteren christlichen Kirche von Malta". *Historisches Jahrbuch,* XVII, 3, 1896, pp. 475-496.

Meinardus, O. "Melita Illyrica or Africana: An Examination of the Site of St. Paul's Shipwreck." *Ostkirchliche Studien,* XXIII, 1, 1974, pp. 21-36.

———. "Cretan Traditions about St. Paul's Mission to the Island." *Ostkirchliche Studien,* XXII, 2-3, 1973, pp. 172-183.

Morton, H.V. *In the Steps of St. Paul.* London, 1963.

Neale, John M. *Notes, Ecclesiological and Picturesque on Dalmatia, etc.* London, 1861.

Niderstedt, Burchard. *Malta vetus et nova.* Helmstadt, 1659.

Ogg, George. *The Odyssey of Paul. A Chronology.* Old Tappan, 1968.

Palunko, V. *Melita nel naufragio di San Paolo e la isola Meleda in Dalmazia.* Spalato, 1910.

Parisi, G. *La Prima dimora di S. Paolo in Roma.* Alba, 1927.

Pfister, Fr. "Die zweimalige römische Gefangenschaft und die spanische Reise des Apostels Paulus". *Zeitschrift für neutestamentliche Wissenschaft,* XIV, 1913, pp. 216-221.

Pirri, R. *Silicia Sacra.* Palermo, 1733.

Ramsay, William Mitchell. "St. Paul's Shipwreck." *The Expositor*, 5, VI, 1897, pp. 170-173.

———. *Luke the Physician and Other Studies in the History of Religion*. London, 1908.

———. *St. Paul the Traveller and the Roman Citizen*. London, 1905.

Ridolfini, Cecilia P. *St. Paul's Outside the Walls*. Rome, 1967.

Serra, Vilaro Juan. *San Pablo en Espana. Commemoracion del XIX Centenario du sa venida*. Tarragona, 1963.

Sevenster, J.N. *Paul and Seneca*. Leiden, 1961.

Sherwin-White, A.N. *Roman Society and Roman Law in the New Testament*. Oxford, 1963.

Smith, James. *The Voyage and Shipwreck of St. Paul*. London, 1856.

Spier. *In historia critica de Hispanic Pauli itinere*. Witembergaae, 1742.

Stuart, James, and Revett, Nicholas. *The Antiquities of Athens*. London, 1762.

Thevenot. *Travels in the Levant*. London, 1687.

Tre Fontane. Abbazia della Tre Fontane, 1967.

Trump, D.H. *Malta, an Archaeological Guide*. London, 1972.

Vega, Angel Custodio. "La venida de San Pablo a Espana y los Varones Apostólicos". *Boletin de la Real Academia de la Historia*, 114, 1964, pp. 7-78.

Villada, Zacarias Gracia. *Historia Eclesiastica de Espana*. Madrid, 1929.

Vimer, R. *Malta ili Mljet*. Zagreb, 1911.

Vives, José. *Tradición y leyenda en la Hagiografía Hispanica*. Barcelona, 1965.

Watkins, Thomas. *Travels through part of Greece, Ragusa and the Dalmatian Isles*. london, 1792.

Wᴀod, C.T. *The Life, Letters and Religion of St. Paul*. Edinburgh, 1925.

Zammit, Loreto. *St. Paul, Christ's Envoy to Malta*. Malta, 1960.

Index

154

In the Footsteps of the Saints
A new series of travel guides

Otto F.A. Meinardus

A new series of inexpensive guides for travellers and others interested in retracing the journeys of early Christian figures. The geographical context of the lands described is supplemented by historical accounts, references to recen archaeological finds and observation about the life and customs of th inhabitants.

Each title is about 160 pages and is available in either a paperback or hardback version; the text is illustrated by many photographs. All books are uniform in format, 5½" x 8¼".
PRICE: $4.95 (paperback)
$7.50 (hardcover)

ST. PAUL IN EPHESUS and the Cities of Galatia and Cyprus
ISBN 0-89241-044-2 (paperback)
0-89241-071-x (hardcover)

ST. PAUL IN GREECE
ISBN 0-89241-045-0 (paperback)
0-89241-072-8 (hardcover)

ST. PAUL'S LAST JOURNEY
ISBN 0-89241-046-9 (paperback)
0-89241-073-6 (hardcover)

ST. JOHN OF PATMOS and the Seve Churches of the Apocalypse.
ISBN 0-89241-043-4 (paperback)
0-89241-070-1 (hardcover)

CARATZAS BROTHERS, PUBLISHERS
246 Pelham Road
New Rochelle, New York 10805